Guinea Pig

Animal
Series editor: Jonathan Burt

Guinea Pig

Dorothy Yamamoto

REAKTION BOOKS

Published by
REAKTION BOOKS LTD
33 Great Sutton Street
London EC1V 0DX, UK
www.reaktionbooks.co.uk

First published 2015
Copyright © Dorothy Yamamoto 2015

Printed and bound in China by C&C Printing Co. Ltd

A catalogue record for this book is available from the British Library

ISBN 978 1 78023 426 7

Contents

1 What's in a Name?

I met literary guinea pigs before I met real ones. One of the bonuses of being ill as a child was that my mother would invariably sit on my bed and read me 'Pigs is Pigs' by the American writer Ellis Parker Butler.[1] In this comic short story, Mike Flannery, agent of the Interurban Express Company, becomes embroiled in a dispute with an irascible customer, Mr Morehouse, over the rate to be charged for transporting a pair of guinea pigs. Mr Morehouse argues he should pay 25 cents as they are 'pets', but Flannery sticks to his rule book and demands 30 cents. "'Pigs is pigs,'" he declared firmly. "Guinea-pigs, or dago pigs or Irish pigs is all the same to the Interurban Express Company an' to Mike Flannery. Th' nationality of the pig creates no differentiality in the rate, Misther Morehouse!'" The row simmers on, involving endless missives from Head Office, and eventually the deal-breaking intervention of a scholarly professor. Meanwhile the guinea pigs, 'eatin' loike ragin' hippypottymusses', have increased in number to several thousand, and the tale ends with Flannery, who has been instructed to return the shipment, shovelling them by the dozen into bushel baskets with a coal scoop.

Despite being treated as commodities, the guinea pigs in 'Pigs is Pigs' succeed in taking over the story, and in completely flummoxing the human characters. At the same time, they remain ambiguous little presences, escaping the net of regulations that is supposed to contain them. Guinea pigs may lack the glamour of wolves or tigers or the mythic resonance of snakes, swans or foxes, but as key participants in numerous human enterprises – from farming and medicine to space travel and the pet industry – they have quietly run alongside us for much of our history, and in doing so have raised important questions about how we characterize, and exploit, the animal world. This book places them centre stage.

Guinea pigs are rodents of the family Caviidae, subfamily Caviinae, genus *Cavia*. The familiar small family pets belong to a distinct species, *C. porcellus*, which (apart from a few feral escapees) does not exist in the wild. Flannery's predicament has been exaggerated for effect: guinea pigs are not nearly as prolific as rabbits, rats or mice, since their relatively long gestation period – 63 to 75 days, about twice the length of a rabbit pregnancy – limits the number of litters that can be born in a year. (However, they reach sexual maturity earlier than other rodents: females can become pregnant when they are about four weeks old, compared

A precocial baby guinea pig (about 8 hours old).

to six weeks for mice and thirteen weeks for rabbits.) The babies emerge fully formed, like miniature adults, and can quickly run about and forage for themselves. This is in keeping with the lifestyle of related wild species, which do not create permanent homes for themselves but rely on nimbleness and anticipation to avoid becoming prey.

The guinea pig's close relatives include *C. aperea*, *C. fulgida* and *C. tschudii*, native to the Andean region of South America (present-day Ecuador, Peru, Bolivia, and the southern part of Colombia). *C. magna*, or the greater guinea pig, is found in Brazil and Uruguay. About 8,000 years ago, rising sea levels isolated the tiny island of Moleques do Sul, off the Brazilian coast, and with it a population of *C. magna*, which evolved into *C. intermedia*, or Santa Catarina's guinea pig, now one of the most critically endangered species on the planet and numbering fewer than 60 individuals in 2012.[2]

Cavia porcellus developed into a distinct species because of selective breeding by the Andean peoples, a history which is discussed more fully in chapter Two. Its ancestor was probably either *C. aperea* or *C. tschudii*.[3] *Porcellus* is Latin for 'little pig', and the 'pig' element has carried over into other languages besides English: the German *Meerschweinchen* ('sea piglet'), French *cochon d'Inde* ('Indian pig'), Dutch *Guinees biggetje* ('Guinea piglet') and Portuguese *porquinho da Índia* ('little Indian pig'). The animal's chunky body, its wheeks and squeals and its habit of eating almost non-stop, certainly prompt the comparison. However, it derives more precisely from the writings of the Spanish historian Gonzalo Fernández de Oviedo y Valdés (or Oviedo, 1478–1557), whose *Historia general y natural de las Indias* ('General and Natural History of the Indies', 1526) chronicled Spain's New World possessions. Oviedo introduced many now familiar plants and animals to European eyes – his book contains, for instance, the first drawing of a pineapple. He met guinea pigs in Santo Domingo, now in the Dominican Republic, where he worked as the supervisor of

The endangered Santa Catarina's guinea pig.

gold smeltings. They are not native to that place, or anywhere in the West Indies or Central America, so they must have been imported from their Andean homeland by pre-Columbian settlers. Oviedo named the new animal *cori* and characterized it as *chanchito de la India*, or 'little pig of the Indies'. It is likely that he had its household role in mind: like full-size pigs, guinea pigs were penned close to the homestead, or actually indoors, and were fattened on leftover scraps before being eaten. Oviedo was favourably impressed by *coris*, which he described as 'like rabbits or young conies. They are not vicious and are very pretty. Some are entirely white, while others are white spotted with red and other colors.' Unlike the lovestruck alleycats that had disturbed his night-time studies in Spain, *coris* were pleasingly quiet: they are 'mute animals and not bothersome, and very tame; they move about the house and keep it clean, and they do not screech or make a noise or gnaw things or do damage'.[4]

'Guinea' is more problematic, since the country of Guinea is on the west coast of Africa, far from guinea pigs' homeland. The word may be a corruption of 'Guiana' ('unlikely', the *Oxford English Dictionary* thinks), or it may simply equate to 'exotic'. However, Guinea was a port of call for the 'Guinea-men', those ships that plied the slave trade from the West African coast to the New World plantations; since such vessels may well have transported guinea pigs on their return voyage to Europe, they provide a plausible explanation for the name. The *OED* does not record 'Guinea-man' until 1695 but, interestingly, it gives as one of its alternative meanings 'one who earns guinea fees (as a juryman)', which is also one of the derivatives of 'guinea pig'. A popular etymology, still occasionally repeated, that traces the name to the old English guinea coin, on the grounds that the little animals originally cost this (very great) amount, is definitely false: guineas were first circulated in 1663 and the *OED*'s first quotation on the topic is from Samuel

Pepys's diary entry for 29 October 1666, whereas the scientist William Harvey was writing about 'Ginny-pigs' ten years earlier, in 1653.[5]

When guinea pigs arrived in Europe in the middle of the sixteenth century, scientists, inspired by the recent discoveries in the New World, were eagerly compiling catalogues of the whole created universe. The Swiss naturalist Conrad Gesner (1516–1565) was the first to describe them, in his monumental *Historiae animalium*. Gesner assigned them the name *cuniculus vel porcellus indicus* ('Indian rabbit or little pig'); he himself kept a pair of pet guinea pigs, which had been given to him by a doctor friend employed by the fabulously wealthy Fugger mercantile family, whose trading contacts no doubt extended to the Americas. He described their diet (grass, fruit, bread and oats) and noted that, unlike rabbits, they gave birth to precocial young. He drew the illustration that accompanies his text: a dignified little animal with delicately crumpled ears.[6]

Gesner's name for the guinea pig was translated into English by Edward Topsell as 'Indian little pig-cony' ('cony', or 'coney', is the older word for 'rabbit', from the Latin *cuniculus*). Topsell's *Historie of Foure-footed Beastes* (1607) has more in common with medieval bestiaries than with modern empirical studies – he tells us that mice are engendered in the earth, and that lemmings graze in the clouds – and he is heavily indebted to earlier writers, mostly Gesner. Topsell informs us, 'I received the picture of this Beast from a certain Noble-man.' In fact, his illustration is a crude copy of Gesner's, and the animal, with its plain rounded ears, looks far less guinea-pig-like.

In the Spanish of Ecuador, Peru and Bolivia, a guinea pig is a *cuy* (plural *cuyes*); in Quechua, the language of the central Andean region, they are *jaca* (pronounced 'haka'). The German-born zoologist Peter Simon Pallas's (1741–1811) label for the genus, *Cavia*, would appear to derive from *cuy*, although the *Oxford English Dictionary* traces a slightly lengthier route through *cabiai*, the name in Galibi, spoken by the native peoples of French Guiana. *Cobaye* is an alternative to *cochon d'Inde* for a guinea pig in French, and the species itself is sometimes called *Cavia cobaya*. However, the more common specific is *porcellus*, first applied by Carl Linnaeus in 1758 and then combined with *Cavia* by Johann Christian Polycarp Erxleben in 1777.

As British scientists became more familiar with guinea pigs, they became less satisfied with their common name, since they were patently not pigs and did not come from Guinea. In 1781 the Welsh naturalist Thomas Pennant identified several species of 'cavy' in his *History of Quadrupeds*, including the capybara, the Patagonian cavy (the mara), and the spotted cavy (the paca). Pennant listed a variety of names for the guinea pig, including Gesner's *cuniculus vel porcellus indicus* and the Comte de Buffon's *cochon d'Inde*. He admitted that he knew nothing about its 'manners

Edward Topsell's 'Indian little pig-cony', 1607.

in a wild state' (he thought it came from Brazil), but he was well acquainted with it as a domestic pet, fed on 'bread, grains, and vegetables'. He gave the guinea pig a new name, the 'restless cavy', after his characterization of it as 'a restless, grunting little animal; perpetually running from corner to corner'.[7] Pennant's coinage gained currency: in 1831 the *List of the Vertebrated Animals Exhibited in the Gardens of the Zoological Society of London* informed its readers that 'These animals are commonly known by the name of Guinea Pigs; but the species is properly denominated the Restless Cavy.' Curiously, since Pennant's term described captive animals that were perpetually in anxious movement because, with their short sight, they could not see from one end of their pen to the other, it then became attached to a wild species, as in the *Encyclopaedia Britannica*'s entry in 1876: 'The Restless Cavy (*Cavia aperea*), found throughout Uruguay and Brazil, is supposed to be the wild form of the Guinea-pig of Europe.' 'Restless cavy' is still defined as 'wild guinea pig' in some modern dictionaries. It is actually quite apposite, since members of *C. aperea* do not settle in one place for long (although they may shelter in the burrows of other animals, or in rock crevices) but roam in groups in search of vegetation, rather like miniature herds of sheep.

The 'cavy' element in Pennant's coinage has persisted as an alternative term for 'guinea pig' to the present day, and is actually favoured as 'more scientific' by societies of fanciers and breeders. However, this perceived gain in dignity is balanced by a loss of precision, for among the members of the family Caviidae are animals, such as the capybara, which are very different from guinea pigs, while even the genus *Cavia* includes all the wild species mentioned at the beginning of this chapter.

So the labels which have been attached to this small animal are an odd configuration of guesswork and misunderstanding. Linguistically, guinea pigs have a tangled history. And as they

A. Radigue, 'The Guinea Pig', hand-coloured print after Buffon, 1764.

14

became better known in Britain, their two-part name entered into an independent life and gave birth to a whole progeny of secondary meanings.

In the eighteenth century, 'guinea pig' was used to mean an inept or inexperienced sailor. In Tobias Smollett's *The Adventures of Roderick Random* (1748) the hero is attacked and press-ganged near Tower Wharf in London. Luckily he has the wit to ask Jack Rattlin, the sailor guarding him, if he knows his uncle, Lieutenant Tom Bowling, who served on the *Thunder*, where Roderick is bound the following day. 'Odds my life!', Jack declares, 'and that I do; and a good seaman he is as ever stepped upon forecastle, and a brave fellow as ever cracked biscuit – none of your Guinea pigs, nor your fresh water, wish-washy, fair-weather fowls'. In the nineteenth century the term was applied to midshipmen, the youngest and most junior officers, who were originally quartered 'amidships'. It is attested by the popular novelist Frederick Marryat, who began his own naval career in this role: in *Poor Jack* (1840), the narrator Tom Saunders and his mentor, the channel pilot Bramble, board an Indiaman to guide it into Plymouth Sound. They are immediately besieged by the whole ship's company, who are avid for the latest news: 'while Bramble was questioned by the captain and passengers, I was attacked by the midshipmen, or guinea-pigs as they are called'. Do these 'guinea pigs' bear any relation to the animals? It is just possible that there is an echo of the presence of live guinea pigs on long sea voyages, where they may have been seen as timid nuisances scampering aimlessly about.

At the end of the eighteenth century, 'guinea pig' became the sobriquet of those fashion-conscious persons who chose to pay for the privilege of wearing hair powder: in order to reduce the enormous national debt and avoid bankruptcy, the prime minister, William Pitt the Younger, levied taxes on a whole range of luxury items, including men's hats, ladies' ribbons and perfumes, carriages, servants, clocks, gold and silver plate, as well as hair powder. From 1786 packets of the powder had to be stamped to show tax had been paid on them ('stamp duty'); from 1795 paper permits were issued instead, at a cost of one guinea a year.[8]

Fitzinger, 'The Guinea Pig', 1867.

One effect was to speed the decline of wigs, which were often liberally powdered (although hair, too, was dusted with a variety of substances, including flour and turmeric).

The collocation 'guinea pigs' derives from the guinea fee and the 'pigtails' targeted by the tax: there is no explicit connection with the animals themselves. However, satirical cartoonists were quick to seize upon the second element to pillory Pitt, who often appears as a bewigged (porcine) pig. In at least one drawing there is also an allusion to actual guinea pigs: Pitt's great adversary, Charles James Fox, holds aloft a board on which a piggish Pitt sits, surrounded by dancing smaller pigs, all of them wearing powdered wigs. Fox, who is a swarthy black boar, pointedly wearing his own hair, sings:

> Here is a long tail Pig and a short tail Pig, and a Pig without ever A Tail. Here are Guinea Pigs and sucking Pigs with a remarkable pretty Guinea Pig that has never a Tail!

The title of the print, 'Buy my pretty Guinea Pigs!', also seems more fitting for guinea pigs, which were hawked round the streets in this way in the nineteenth century, and possibly earlier. In a nice rounding of the circle, from the 1990s 'guinea pig' has been recorded as Cockney rhyming slang for 'wig': the guinea coin has been forgotten but the rhyme has been recycled, and with it perhaps the image of a guinea pig perched on someone's head like a badly fitting wig.[9]

Reverting to the coin, 'guinea pig' appears from the early nineteenth century onwards as a somewhat derogatory term for someone – a doctor, a vet or a clergyman, for instance – who charges a guinea fee for his services. According to *Chambers's Journal* for 1 May 1858 it was also used for members of a jury: Lewis Carroll probably had this in mind when he included two actual guinea

A dandified human 'guinea pig' holding up a licence to wear hair powder, 1795.

pigs among the jurors hearing the case of 'Who Stole the Tarts?' in *Alice's Adventures in Wonderland* (1865). Some 'guinea pigs' of course earned their fee, but the usage spread to those who put in the minimum effort for the maximum reward: typically a man who 'lives by getting himself placed upon the Boards of a number of companies whose business he can have neither the time nor

Buy my pretty Guinea Pigs

the qualifications to assist in directing'.[10] The *Oxford English Dictionary* also records the verb 'to guinea-pig', which is to indulge in these acquisitive practices. The picture of compliant and well-fed 'gentlemen of more rank than means . . . who have a guinea and a copious lunch when they attend board meetings', as the *Temple Bar* journal for 1871 describes them, perhaps also refracts popular ideas of real guinea pigs: certainly the usage persisted into the twentieth century, and the latest edition of *The Chambers Dictionary* (2011) still lists one of the senses of 'guinea pig' as 'a do-nothing, token company director'.

During the Second World War, men and women who were evacuated from the cities to the countryside, and soldiers who were billeted with civilians, were popularly known as 'guinea pigs'. The reference was ostensibly to the billeting allowance, which was about a guinea, but real guinea pigs crept into the comparison too, as in the complaint of one correspondent in the *Daily Dispatch* of 10 October 1939: 'We are known here as the *guinea-pigs* . . . and we are being treated locally like those tailless rodents.' On 16 July 1940 a journalist on the *Manchester Evening News* found 'every other house' in that city 'teeming with *guinea-pigs*' (that is, soldiers). Guinea pigs, of course, have been typecast as phenomenally rapid breeders, and it is this characteristic that is being alluded to, along with a sense of people being pushed around en masse and treated without proper respect.

The best-known secondary sense of 'guinea pig' is 'the subject of an experiment', whether a person, animal or thing. Guinea pigs were experimented on by scientists from the seventeenth century onwards (see chapter Five), but their name was not used in this way until the early twentieth century (the *OED*'s first citation is from 1913). The usage is now so widespread that it has probably perpetuated the idea that guinea pigs are the commonest laboratory animal, which is no longer the case.

'Buy my pretty Guinea Pigs!', a satirical print of William Pitt and Charles James Fox, 1795.

SEE, SEE, THE GUINEA PIG.
A Study in Profitable Local Self Government.

In 1941 the Guinea Pig Club was founded in East Grinstead, Sussex. Its members were pilots and crew members from the Allied airforce who had been badly burned during service and were receiving treatment at the town's Queen Victoria Hospital (or the 'Sty', as they called it) from the pioneering plastic surgeon Sir Archibald McIndoe. The club started off as a drinking club and retained an atmosphere of boisterous irreverence, effectively sticking two fingers up at those who had written off men who were seriously disfigured, or who shied away from them in public. Sir Archibald, as well as performing many innovative surgical reconstructions, involved himself thoroughly in the lives of his 'Guinea Pigs', allowing barrels of beer to be brought into the hospital wards and forging links between patients and local families in East Grinstead, which became known as 'the town that did not stare'.[11]

Although most of the original Guinea Pigs have now died, the club still meets, and continues its work of helping burns sufferers. The Falklands War veteran Simon Weston is an honorary member. For many years reunions took place at a pub in East Grinstead called The Guinea Pig; the pub closed in 2008, and was demolished to make room for social housing, but its name lives on in the new development's Guinea Pig Place.

McIndoe's Guinea Pigs were experimented on, in one sense, but they chose to define themselves as absolute opposites to passive laboratory specimens. Their badge was a small silver-winged guinea pig, and their 'anthem', written by one of their number, Sergeant Edward 'Blackie' Blacksell, re-echoed their defiance:

We are McIndoe's army,
We are his Guinea Pigs.
With dermatomes and pedicles,
Glass eyes, false teeth and wigs.

The first issue of the Guinea Pig Club's magazine, c. 1941. The bottle of beer on the left (Spitfire Ale) is from 2007 and commemorates the Club's last formal reunion in 1941.

P.J. OLDREIVE

THE GUINEA PIG

And when we get our discharge
We'll shout with all our might:
'*Per ardua ad astra*'
We'd rather drink than fight.

So, the naming of guinea pigs is no simple matter. 'Why do they call me "guinea pig" anyway? I'm not Italian, and I'm not pork!', protests the garrulous guinea pig Rodney in the Eddie Murphy film *Dr Dolittle* (1998), stirring yet another ingredient into the mix, as 'ginny' is derogatory slang for 'Italian'. The twists and turns in the guinea pig's linguistic history reflect its accommodation within European culture; even today 'guinea pig' and 'cavy' are not absolutely synonymous, since they point to different practices, different ways of objectifying the animal. There are also many figurative guinea pigs, from sailors and wig-wearers to jurymen, evacuees and laboratory subjects. These references are usually belittling, suggesting incompetence or passivity. It took 'McIndoe's army' to show that guinea pigs can fight back. The next chapter travels to their Andean homeland, and to the beginnings of their long and transformative association with humans.

The sign from The Guinea Pig pub in East Grinstead, where the Guinea Pig Club once met.

2 At Home in the Andes

Guinea pigs may have been domesticated as early as 5000 BC by tribes living in the Altiplano region of southern Peru and Bolivia. Archaeologists have found burned bones and bones with cut marks in midden deposits from about this time. Their bones have also been found in temples, such as the Temple of the Crossed Hands at Kotosh (c. 2500–2000 BC),[1] or the Gallery of the Offerings in the Old Temple at Chavín de Huántar (c. 1000–500 BC). In the residential district at Chavín, guinea pig bones and *Spondylus* oyster shells lay together under the floor and wall of a house. Spondylid oysters (*mullu* in Quechua) were seen as the food of the gods and were used in rain-making ceremonies; their value is shown by the fact that they were traded many miles inland, appearing in high-status graves – again, sometimes in association with guinea pig bones – in the highlands of what is now Ecuador.[2]

Near Huarmey, on the north-central coast of Peru, stone-lined tunnels in which guinea pigs were kept have been discovered, running between pairs of rooms within houses. The tunnels date to between 2800 and 1500 BC and are filled with a sediment consisting of the remains of the guinea pigs and of anchovies, which they may have been fed by their fisherfolk owners. An alternative explanation identifies these tunnels as ventilation shafts for ritual hearths; however, even if the guinea pigs were

used in rituals, it is very likely that they were also eaten, and the abundant protein that they supplied may explain the relative density of settlement in this area.[3]

The Moche people, who inhabited the arid north coastal region of Peru from about AD 100 to 750, and built the massive, still-standing pyramidal structures of Huaca de la Luna and Huaca del Sol at Cerro Blanco, certainly farmed guinea pigs as well as llamas and turkeys. The remains of pens where the guinea pigs were kept have been identified next to areas of the houses equipped with hearths and grindstones for food preparation.[4]

There is much more evidence for the ritual use of guinea pigs, in the shape of remains in tombs or in temples, than there is for their farming and consumption. The hard architecture of the pens built by the Moche, and the stone tunnels with their preserved contents, at Huarmey, are exceptional survivals: more usually the life cycle of guinea pigs raised for food has left no trace at all. This was shown by two Peruvian archaeologists who investigated a site at which they knew guinea pigs had been reared from the 1930s to the early 1980s. They found no material that revealed this; the explanation was provided by the woman – their aunt – who now lived there, and served them a meal consisting of two fat guinea pigs:

> all the bones were kept until everyone had finished and then placed on the patio for the three dogs to share. In a very few minutes all the greasy, fragile bones had been entirely eaten by the dogs; inspection of the patio did not locate a single piece of guinea pig bone.[5]

The scenario was doubtless very similar centuries ago, so the fact that there is little archaeological evidence for the raising and eating of guinea pigs does not mean that the Andean peoples only occasionally exploited them as a food source. Written accounts from the time of the Spanish conquest suggest the opposite.

Guinea pig remains from the later prehistoric period onwards (from about 200 BC to the sixteenth century AD) have quite frequently been found in ritual contexts. Their bones, together with those of other animals, such as dogs and llamas and various birds, have been unearthed among the tombs of Huaca de la Luna, and at Sipan, where the skeleton of a guinea pig lay on top of the coffin of an adult male.[6] In the urban quarter of Moche, the bodies of three guinea pigs were discovered lying close to the body of a young child, one at the head, one on the right side and a third next to the pelvis: one theory is that they were intended to accompany her (or him) to the other world and provide nourishment there. It has also been suggested that the position of the animals may reflect the therapeutic rubbing of a patient's body with live guinea pigs that is still practised by traditional healers, or *curanderos*.

A burial horde of at least 23 guinea pigs at Cahuachi, dated to the first few centuries AD,

> consist[ed] of disarticulated and disarticulating bodies, whose heads had been jerked off and whose stomach appears to have been slit open by a long incision which extends to the thorax . . . all appear to be young individuals.[7]

Remains of guinea pigs were also found at the great religious centre of Pachacamac (*c*. AD 1000) on the Pacific coast of Peru, about 19 miles (30 km) from Lima. A 'great quantity of guinea pigs wrapped in coverings of maize and achira [the canna lily]' was discovered just below the summit of the Pachacamac Temple.[8] More lay in a burial chamber, which excited interest because it also contained more than 80 human mummies, including the remains of a dozen infants which had been placed around the perimeter of the tomb. Archaeologists can only speculate about the meaning of such positioning: some think a sacrificial ceremony may have taken place here, while others suggest the site may have been a centre for healing, since several of the human bodies showed signs of illness.

In dry desert conditions, natural mummification of bodies can take place, and in a few cases guinea pigs have been preserved in this way, offering us a few more – although still tantalizingly cryptic – clues about their role. A single mummified guinea pig, *c*. AD 300–700, was discovered at the northern Chile site of Punta Pichalo. It was grey-brown with a yellowish belly and a distinctive line of black hair running from above the eyes to the nose

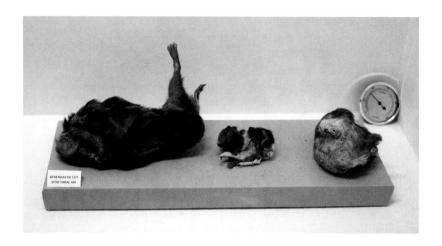

and mouth. The body was intact, and tied round its neck was a brown thread of llama or alpaca wool, with a red flamingo feather.[9]

At El Yaral, a site occupied by the Chiribaya people in the valley of Moquegua, southern Peru, *c*. AD 1000, archaeologists discovered the bodies of about 70 sacrificed guinea pigs. The heads had been removed and placed above or beneath each individual, while several had damage to the cervical vertebrae, showing how they had been killed. The state of preservation was so good that coat colours could be distinguished: brown, chestnut and orange piebald.[10] X-rays revealed small compacted masses inside some of the animals' mouths – possibly wads of coca leaves, which have been found in the mouths of mummified guinea pigs from the Moche valley.

Detailed investigation of the 'size, hair color and design polymorphisms, and lower skulls' of these mummified specimens 'demonstrated that [guinea pigs] were fully domesticated in southern Peru–northern Chile more than 500 years before the arrival of the Spaniards to the Americas'. When a wild species is domesticated, the physical changes that are induced tend to follow a common pattern: 'increase in body size and fertility, pelage polymorphisms, changes in the color and size of eyes, ears, and face, reduction of brain size and dentition, redistribution of body fat, and behavioral changes'. Such characteristics were typical of the El Yaral and Punta Pichalo guinea pigs: variegated coat colours, a smaller brain and a larger body size (although this last was harder to be sure of, as many of the animals, like those at Cahuachi, were juveniles).[11]

At the Inca period (c. AD 1480–1540) fishing settlement of Lo Demás, about 200 km south of Lima in the Chincha valley, archaeologists have discovered guinea pig faeces, separated bones (often charred or gnawed) and naturally mummified bodies, bringing together the whole spectrum of utilization within that society. At least one animal had been sacrificed by slitting the stomach lengthwise; another accompanied the burial of a child, lying underneath the reed mat on which the child's wrapped body had been placed. A midden contained both the remains of guinea pigs and the fibres of medicinal plants; similar plant fibres were found in the stomach of an adult burial associated with that of the child, perhaps suggesting that a *curandero* was at work here.[12]

The Andean peoples had no written language; however, when the Spanish conquistadors arrived, their chroniclers set down many instances of guinea pig symbolism and use which must reach back several centuries and therefore shed light retrospectively on some of the archaeological findings. In 1559, for instance, the government official Juan Polo de Ondegardo described the natives' practice of slitting open guinea pigs to study their entrails for good or bad omens.[13] It was their principle only to sacrifice domestic animals, which had been imprinted with human labour, and so these were tame, not wild, cavies. The missionary Father Pablo José de Arriaga observed, in 1621:

> The ordinary sacrifice is of guinea pigs, of which they make evil use, not only for sacrifices but also to divine with them and to cure with them . . . When they have to sacrifice them, sometimes they open them along the middle with the nail of the thumb.[14]

Father Bernabé Cobo travelled widely in the Andes during the first half of the seventeenth century and viewed the keeping of guinea pigs at first hand:

> The guinea pig is the smallest of the domestic animals that the natives of these Indies had; they bred it in their houses and centers, as they do today. It is little bigger than a rat . . . [but] it lacks a tail. There are guinea pigs of many colors . . . They have a low voice, which makes a noise like a child that cries or moans, although when they are grabbed, they give more strident squeals.[15]

Cobo noted that guinea pig was a favoured food among the Indians and described a method of cooking in which, after evisceration, the animal's body cavity was filled with smooth pebbles to speed up the roasting process.[16] He also recorded the role of guinea pigs in healing practices: 'It was also customary to cure [patients] by rubbing and sucking the sick man's abdomen and other parts of his body while smearing the same parts with grease or the meat and fat of the *cui* or of a toad.'[17]

The tradition mentioned by Cobo of keeping guinea pigs inside the house (which survives to this day) is also alluded to by the chronicler Felipe Guaman Poma de Ayala, a descendant of

Inca nobility, who wrote his major work, *The First New Chronicle and Good Government* (*c*. 1615), in order to show the Spanish king that the native 'Indians' were being exploited by the colonial government and had fared much better under their indigenous rulers. Guaman Poma records numerous aspects of Inca culture, including twice-yearly inspections (in June and December) by royal officials to make sure that every dwelling in the kingdom was well stocked with provisions: 'they even check each house for domestic cavies, ducks and livestock'.[18] In July the inspectors moved on to the *chacras*, or cultivated fields, allotting a certain proportion to communal ownership:

> At this time a sacrifice was made of one hundred reddish-brown llamas [or 'llamas decorated with a red sash']. The llamas were burned in the public square along with a thousand white *cuis* [guinea pigs]. This sacrifice was performed so that the sun and the rains would not damage the crops in the *chacras*.[19]

The whiteness of the *cuis* suggests that the Incas had worked out some of the rules of genetic inheritance, since this coat colour (excepting albinism) does not occur in wild populations. Guinea pigs were also sacrificed in August, when the maize was planted. Guaman Poma illustrated his chronicle with numerous drawings: one of these shows a guinea pig being lifted up and offered to a *huaca*, or deity.

After the fall of the Inca empire, Spanish adventurers penetrated deeper into the continent in their frenzied search for gold. One of their targets was the immensely rich Muisca or Chibcha Andean kingdom, near present-day Bogotá in Colombia. An expedition led by the lawyer Gonzalo Jiménez de Quesada was the first to arrive there, in 1537, after enduring tremendous hardships and enlos condes

the loss of many men. The Muisca evidently reared guinea pigs intensively, for they attempted to appease the godlike strangers by supplying them with up to a thousand animals a day, together with an abundance of deer meat.[20] Despite this, relations worsened and hostilities broke out, resulting in the torture and killing of the Muisca rulers by the invaders. Later, during the Vilcabamba campaign to capture the last Inca stronghold, the Spanish would occasionally find sacrificed guinea pigs lying in their path in an attempt to deflect them from their goal.[21]

The ritual use of guinea pigs obviously ran counter to the new religion that the conquistadors brought to the continent, and in the sixteenth century their priests appealed to the archbishop of Lima, asking him to order their complete extermin- ation.[22] Fortunately, Archbishop Loayza refused their request, 'for fear of a general rebellion', and the guinea pigs survived,

A guinea pig is lifted up and offered to an Inca deity, from Felipe Guaman Poma, *The First New Chronicle and Good Government* (c. 1615).

Detail showing the offered guinea pig.

Jesus and the Apostles eat guinea pig: Marcos Zapata's *Last Supper*, c. 1753.

to be incorporated into the mix of Christian and indigenous traditions which now characterized the region. In fact, Edmundo Morales has suggested that acceptance by the Spanish of the practical and symbolic significance of guinea pigs within the native culture made it easier for the two worlds to coexist.[23] An example is provided by the Escuela Cusqueña (Cusco School of Art), which was established in order to educate local artists in European painting traditions, specifically of religious subjects. While these artists faithfully followed their models, they also found ways of including native iconography in their work, as in Marcos Zapata's *Last Supper* in the cathedral of Santo Domingo, Cusco, which shows Jesus and the disciples gathered around a platter of roasted guinea pig and sharing bottles of *chicha* beer, brewed from fermented maize.[24] The fact that, unlike the paschal lamb, one guinea pig would hardly feed thirteen people actually underlines its status as a symbolic food, eaten on ceremonial occasions or offered to honoured guests. According to Cusco tradition, the figure of Judas Iscariot, who turns away from the communal table to stare directly at us, is a portrait of the conquistador Francisco Pizarro.

Guinea pigs have retained their special place in the economy of the Andean peoples. Unlike other farmed animals, such as llamas, their traditional home is inside the house, often in the kitchen, where the smoky atmosphere is said to improve their flavour, and a low doorsill keeps them from straying. Sometimes special cubbyholes (*cuyeros*) in which they can sleep or give birth are constructed for them 'of rock or adobe, usually under the hearth or in a corner'.[25] They thus belong 'to a private world . . . to a closed rather than a public space' and also to 'the world of female domestic practices', since it is the task of the women to take care of them, feeding them inexpensively on alfalfa and vegetable peelings (or even ripe bananas, in the areas where these are grown). Although they are certainly not pets – they are not given names – their presence helps to define the domestic realm, so that 'A peasant house without guinea pigs is not . . . a complete home'. They are seen as timid creatures, much in need of the warmth of the hearth ('too stupid to be left outside', according to one Ecuadorian informant), and they are thought to be particularly sensitive to the presence of 'strangers'. The miscarriages of pregnant guinea pigs are sometimes attributed to the fright caused by intruders, whether humans or other animals, such as dogs, cats, rats or the *chuchuri*, a member of the weasel family which is supposed to have a desperate craving for guinea pig meat.[26]

Certainly guinea pigs make up part of a family's wealth, and they can be sold for money, either in markets or within the immediate community, but they are more frequently presented as gifts on special occasions, to affirm family ties or to mark an anniversary. In Peru the hair-cutting ceremony called *rutichico* goes back to Inca times, and was recently witnessed by Quin Murray in a small village called Chaquepay, about two hours' travel from Cusco. An eight-year-old girl was having her hair cut for the first time, and her mother and father had chosen godparents for her; it was expected that the godparents would give her a present – typically a few guinea pigs as a sort of 'starter' herd.[27] Edmundo Morales describes the presentation of guinea pigs at a betrothal (which sadly went wrong, as too much beer was drunk and the groom ended up sleeping with the wrong sister), and he also notes the refrain of a Quechua folksong: 'Hey old lady, if you want me to be your son-in-law, open your door and serve me a whole *cuy*.'[28]

As the song hints, such festivities involved the eating of guinea pigs too. When an important guest was entertained, members of the household, especially women and children, would be served last, perhaps receiving no more than the fried blood mixed with boiled potatoes. Guinea pigs are eaten more widely now than they used to be, especially after the Peruvian government's attempts to promote their husbandry as a way for peasant families to improve their standard of living, but another of Quin Murray's observations shows that they are still associated with the seasonal rituals of the farming year. In Chaquepay, guinea pigs that had spent the previous few months being fattened up were killed just before the fields were ploughed and seeded. The ploughing was done by groups of eight men, who moved round the fields in turn and were fed each day by the wife of the man whose field they were working. It was her task to kill the guinea pigs (by quickly wringing their necks) and prepare the feast.

A guinea pig is quickly killed for a feast to celebrate ploughing the fields, in Chaquepay, Peru.

38

Guinea pigs are also used in healing rituals performed by *curanderos*, or folk doctors, in many parts of the Andes. They are seen as particularly appropriate for this because of their close proximity to humans: 'it lives in the house', 'it has been living with people for a long time', 'it is a very well-known animal' and 'it is a favoured animal' were some of the answers people gave when they were asked why the guinea pig was special.[29] To diagnose an illness, the healer may rub a guinea pig all over the patient's body and then kill the animal and dissect the corpse, looking for signs of abnormality. For example, a throat infection may be indicated by clotted blood in the neck, or colic by air bubbles in the intestines. Black guinea pigs (which are quite rare, and expensive to buy) are often specified, and patients are expected to bring their own.

Edmundo Morales witnessed several healing episodes involving guinea pigs in the course of his research for his book on their role in Andean society. He watched one well-known Ecuadorian healer, Juan Carhua, treat an old man; the *curandero* first sat in silence, with his eyes closed, for about a minute, 'as if he were meditating':

> He held the black cuy gently and sprayed perfumed water on the patient's body and began rubbing him. The patient was declared to have been cleaned from 'bad humor he had absorbed somewhere from someone'.[30]

In this case the animal was not killed; instead it acted as a proxy, taking the patient's malady into itself. This was also the idea behind the work of another healer observed by Morales, Marcos Quishuar. The tools of Quishuar's calling – small rocks, a thin bone and guinea pigs – all had some relation to the nearby sacred mountain, Quinchi Urco, and it was the mountain's natural force

Hutches for guinea pigs in a traditional Peruvian home.

that he aimed to appease in the rituals that he performed. For example, with child patients,

> The parent or guardian brings an unwashed cloth or diaper that the sick child has been wearing for the last day or so. The curandero covers the cuy with the child's cloth as if he were draping a doll, which he then fastens with ribbons and yarns of various colours. The parent's or relatives' mission is to take the cuy that has absorbed the *susto* ['fright', nervousness] from the child's body to Quinchi Urco and abandon it there.[31]

The best time to leave the guinea pig on the mountain is late evening or at night. The practice has produced a small feral population on Quinchi Urco which, according to tradition, is herded by the ancestral spirits of the community.

The sense that the guinea pig's body is not just a tool but is to be respected as a conduit for the forces of nature is also apparent when the animal is not released unharmed but is sacrificed for diagnosis. Morales watched a *curandera*, Antonia, treat a ten-year-old boy by rubbing him with a guinea pig and then killing it, skinning it and submerging it in a bowl of water. The trembling of the flesh and the appearance of a thin white membrane indicated that the boy had been suffering from *susto*, which the guinea pig had now taken from him. Afterwards Antonia followed a precise etiquette for disposal of the animal's body, first replacing its skin and then wrapping it carefully in a piece of paper, together with the fresh flowers she had also used to treat her patient. On her way home she placed the wrapped guinea pig in among the spiky leaves of an agave plant, which would protect it from being eaten by predators.[32]

Guinea pigs are used to cure minor complaints by ordinary people as well as by designated healers. When Morales ordered one in a restaurant in Cochabamba, Bolivia, he was asked by the owner if he wanted the cooking liquid to use as medicine. It was supposed to be an exemplary hair tonic: the restaurant owner brought out one of her employees, who had previously been losing her hair, as proof. And a folk remedy for styes is to apply a fresh, warm guinea pig dropping, pressing it on to the eyelid.[33]

The *jaca tsariy* ('gathering of the guinea pigs') is a traditional festivity that takes place in the province of Antonio Raimondi in northern Peru. It happens around the day of the local patron saint, and is a further example of how Andean culture has appropriated the Christian beliefs and practices imposed after the Spanish conquest. The sponsor of the celebrations, the *mayordomo* or *prioste*, issues invitations to attend the feast to women of the community (*llumtsuys*, 'daughters-in-law'), who are then visited in turn one night by a lively procession so that

Guinea pigs forage beneath a stack of corncobs in Peru.

43

they can deliver up their guinea pigs with due ceremony. As Edmundo Morales describes it,

> [The group goes] to each and every *llumtsuy*'s door to dance and whistle to the rhythm of the songs played by the band and to drink chicha, alcohol, and *huarapo* (fermented sugar cane drink). The *llumtsuys* come out of their houses proudly holding a tray of *cuy* meal (*jaca pichu*) and showing an elegantly adorned live *cuy* held by an appointed *torero* [bull-fighter]. The sponsor then welcomes them with firecrackers, and the band begins playing a marchlike song that indicates the departure for another *llumtsuy*'s house. The *jaca toreros* go dancing alongside the *llumtsuys*, and from time to time they place their bull (*cuy*) on the floor to scare people. The *cuy* is tied to the *torero*'s hand with a cord or ribbon.[34]

At the feast itself the *jaca toreros* keep the guests amused by sneaking their little 'bulls' under women's dresses or placing them on their laps, while the cooked guinea pigs on trays are used to poke fun at figures of authority, such as politicians or absentee landlords, as the master of ceremonies picks them up in turn, calling each by a particular person's name. That person's death is then declared and his will read out before his 'body' is handed over to be cut up and shared round the audience.

As Morales says, the *jaca tsariy* ritual has a complex of meanings. First and foremost it acts to bind kinship networks together by involving everyone in rituals of reciprocity, as food and drink are exchanged and consumed. It is also an expression of social satire, both in the mocking of local notables through the dead guinea pigs' bodies, and in the 'gathering' itself, which parodies the collection of tributes by the Spanish conquistadors and, later, the imposition of tithes to support the Church.

In other parts of the Andes, too, guinea pigs appear in the context of religious celebrations. For example, in Pujili, in the province of Cotopaxi, Ecuador, on the feast of Octava, the day after Corpus Christi, tall poles are erected, the crossbars hung with prizes that always include guinea pigs, usually white ones. Local boys and young men try to scale the poles, which are sometimes greased to make climbing difficult, in order to grab a prize.[35] In some indigenous communities in Ecuador roasted guinea pigs are hung up in a 'castle' (a small shed) as offerings to the Magi, who visit at Epiphany. And pilgrims to distant shrines invariably

Guinea pigs in their 'castle' in Caracoto, Peru.

pack the meat among their provisions after making an offering of guinea pigs to the Virgin or another saint before setting out.[36]

In an annual celebration in Churin, Peru, guinea pigs are paraded in elaborate handmade costumes and prizes are awarded for the biggest, the best dressed and the tastiest.

It is not surprising either that there are a number of games and beliefs involving guinea pigs. In Bolivia, drinking companions 'nibble the fried head of the *cuy* and crack the skull to pick out the two tiny bones of the eardrum'. One bone (or *zorro*, 'fox') is slightly bigger than the other; both are dropped in a glass of beer, and their movements as the beer is drunk are carefully noted. The larger bone represents the man, the smaller the woman: if either drifts away from the other it means that he or she is cheating on their partner. In Peru, the 'foxes' game is not used for fortune telling but is simply a drinking contest: the *zorro* is dropped in a glass of wine or beer and the challenge is to remove it with one's lips. Failure to do so means buying everyone another round. Travellers in the Andes carry a guinea pig foot as an amulet, or offer the skulls of guinea pigs, together with quids of coca, to the spirits of the mountains so that they and their packs may be protected against storms and lightning.[37]

Guinea pigs therefore occupy a special place in Andean society. Yet the role of these little spirits of the hearth is inevitably changing as the forces of modernization reach previously remote areas. In Peru, for example, the building of the Trans-oceanic highway has recently been completed. This road leads from the Nazca lines, south of Lima, through the heartland of traditional Andean culture in southeast Peru, and across the lowlands of Bolivia and central Brazil before reaching the Atlantic Ocean, which it now links with the Pacific. The result is bound to be migration to nearby towns and cities, and a closer acquaintance with the values and practices of the industrialized world, with its lightning pathways

Gourd carved as a guinea pig by Andean craftspeople.

46

of communication. There are new developments in guinea pig husbandry, in which the animals are farmed commercially for direct economic benefit. Modern medicine, too, is challenging the traditional remedies: according to Edmundo Morales, people will walk for hours to the nearest population centre to buy very basic, over-the-counter drugs. The *curanderos* still offer an alternative, but whether their work will survive the onset of modernization is far from certain.

3 Arriving in Europe

Guinea pigs travelled to Europe in the mid-sixteenth century aboard the ships of Spanish, Dutch and English traders. It is likely that they provided a welcome source of fresh meat on the long sea voyage; some, however, survived, and were taken up as exotic pets by royalty and the nobility. Elizabeth I is reputed to have owned one and, intriguingly, a richly dressed young girl (aged seven: '*aetatis 7*') in a triple portrait of about 1580 is shown holding a smooth-haired ginger and white guinea pig. She is standing between two young boys – presumably her brothers – one of whom clasps a small bird, perhaps a linnet. The style of embroidery on the boys' collars is certainly English, although the picture itself may have been painted by a Dutch artist, or one at least familiar with Dutch techniques.[1] Guinea pigs were also acquired and experimented on by scientists such as William Harvey.

Only a few skeletal remains have been found in Europe by archaeologists, which is not surprising given their fragility. However, guinea pig bones dating from about 1575 were discovered during excavations at Hill Hall in Theydon Mount, Essex. The house was then occupied by Thomas Smith (1512–1577), a scholar and statesman who rose from humble beginnings – he was the son of a sheep farmer in Saffron Walden – to become Vice-Chancellor of Cambridge University and Secretary of State

ÆTATIS·SVE·6· ÆTATIS·7· ÆTATIS·SVE·5·

during Edward VI's minority. This guinea pig was not played with by Thomas's children, for he had none; he was a man of wide interests and perhaps valued it as a curiosity.[2]

Elizabethan portrait of three children with a guinea pig, c. 1580, artist unknown.

More evidence is available about the guinea pig skeleton unearthed from the infill of a cellar in Mons, Belgium, in 2007, and dated to the end of the sixteenth or beginning of the seventeenth century. Isotope analysis of the animal's bones showed that it had been fed on table scraps, not maize, as an Andean guinea pig would have been, so in all likelihood it was born and raised in Europe. Its skeleton was complete, not dismembered, and bore no traces of knife marks or butchery, suggesting that it was not kept for food but as a family pet. We know little about its

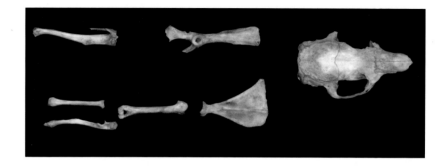

The bones of the Mons guinea pig.

owners, but fragments of ceramics and glassware point to a burgher household, a notch or two down from the aristocracy.[3]

The painter Jan Brueghel the Elder (1568–1625) frequently included a pair of guinea pigs in his biblical and mythological works – two particular animals, in fact, become a kind of running motif. Brueghel's earliest attempt at a guinea pig, however, in *The Garden of Eden with the Fall of Man*, on which he collaborated with Hendrick de Clerck, was clearly not drawn from life – it looks like a scaled-down sheep. It is succeeded by two far more lifelike animals in his *Venus and Cupid* (with Hendrick van Balen), who sit at the feet of the goddess, next to a bowl overflowing with grapes.

From 1606 to 1621 Brueghel was court painter to Infanta Isabella of Spain and her husband, Archduke Albert of Austria, joint rulers of the Spanish Netherlands and avid collectors of exotic animals and birds. We know that Brueghel studied the animals in their Brussels menagerie from a letter he wrote to his patron, Cardinal Borromeo, in 1621, and we also know that, in 1612, the archducal couple purchased 'nineteen parakeets and three guinea pigs'.[4] However, the artist's native town of Antwerp was a vibrant port through which many of the newfound creatures from the Americas were traded, and he may equally well have made his observations closer to home. In *The Entry of the Animals into Noah's Ark* a pair of guinea pigs appear in the foreground, peaceably nibbling pea pods. Near them are crested porcupines, turkeys and a chipmunk, fellow imports from the New World. Although the Ark stands ready to receive its guests, there is no sense of impending doom among the multitude of animals who pose, stretch, prowl or pace in a paradisal landscape. The painting celebrates 'the abundance and variety of species created and preserved by the hand of God',[5] as well as the years of peace in which it was painted (the guinea pigs do not appear at all fazed by the snarling lions immediately behind them).

The *Noah's Ark* guinea pigs are distinctively marked. One is mostly ginger, with a black head and forequarters and white-striped nose, while its companion is slightly paler, with a patchily black and white face and a dark, irregular band encircling its back. The same two reappear in *The Temptation of Adam and Eve, The Sense of Smell, The Madonna and Child in a Garland* and in several

Jan Brueghel the Elder, *The Entry of the Animals into Noah's Ark*, 1613, detail.

51

Jan Brueghel the Elder and Peter Paul Rubens, *The Return from War: Mars Disarmed by Venus*, c. 1610–12.

paintings in which Brueghel collaborated with his great friend Peter Paul Rubens, including *The Return from War: Mars Disarmed by Venus*, *The Garden of Eden with the Fall of Man* and *Flora and Zephyr*.

In *The Return from War*, 'Venus divests her returning lover of his armor as he stands relaxed and oblivious to her cupids playfully stealing away his martial emblems'.[6] The picture is generally agreed to refer to the Twelve Years' Truce of 1609, which had been brokered by Brueghel's patron, Archduke Albert, and brought hostilities between the Protestant northern provinces and the Catholic southern Netherlands to a halt. In the foreground are two guinea pigs, reflecting in their small way the happy union of the divine lovers. One critic has characterized them as 'the exotic embodiment of fruitfulness that accompanies Peace'.[7] The warm earth colour of the imprimatura is used for the shades of their coats, incorporating them fully into the scene. They are certainly the pair we have met before, but they are now eating leaves instead of pea pods. Does this familiarity with their diet, together with the meticulous attention to detail that picks out even individual hairs, suggest that these animals were not observed in the Archduke's menagerie, but were the painter's own pets? It is a tempting theory.

Brueghel and Rubens, *The Return from War*, detail.

During the seventeenth and eighteenth centuries, guinea pigs appear as modish accessories for ladies of fashion. In *The Guardian* (1713), Joseph Addison and Richard Steele's briefly published successor to *The Tatler*, a lovelorn correspondent has a dream in which he is magically able to see every thought in his mistress's heart. Fans, silks, ribbons and laces lie thick together, and are followed by coaches, hands of cards, playhouses and puppet shows. An hour's attention is devoted to 'a Pair of new Shoes', then these give way to 'a Lap-dog, who was succeeded by a *Guiney* pig, a Squirrill and a Monkey. I my self, to my no small Joy, brought up the Rear of these worthy Favourites.'[8]

In 1760 the English naturalist George Edwards described the guinea pig in the second volume of his *Gleanings of Natural History*:

> The GUINEY-PIG is rather bigger than our English Squirrel; its teeth are like those of a Rabbet: it hath small round ears: there are four toes on each of the fore feet: it is without a tail. Its colour is mostly white; but they are spotted more or less with carrot-colour and black, in great variety, no two of them being marked alike. They are bred tame about London, and feed like Rabbets.[9]

Edwards's real interest, however, was in birds (he has been called the 'father of British ornithology'), and his picture of a guinea pig ('drawn from life') next to the mighty dodo functions as a sort of scale model, 'to give a true idea of its [the dodo's] magnitude'.[10]

The Anglo-Irish writer Oliver Goldsmith considered that the guinea pig 'has been so long rendered domestic, and so widely diffused, that it is now become common in every part of the world'. Goldsmith's *A History of the Earth and Animated Nature*, published posthumously in 1774, is a glorious ragbag of fact and fiction, largely drawn from the works of earlier naturalists such as the Comte de Buffon, Carl Linnaeus and John Ray. His entry on the guinea pig, which comes in the section 'Animals of the Hare Kind', confirms its popularity among ladies: 'in some places

David de Coninck,
*Ducks, Guinea Pigs
and a Rabbit in a
Wooded Landscape
beside a Lake,*
c. 1644.

George Edwards,
*Dodo and Guinea
Pig,* 1757.

it . . . is often found even to displace the lap-dog.' The article contains a number of close observations of guinea pig behaviour, such as their liking for 'new milk', their tendency to gnaw 'cloaths, paper, or whatever of this kind they meet with' and their habit of familial grooming: 'The male and female take this office by turns; and when they have thus brushed up each other, they then bestow all their concern upon their young, taking particular care to make their hair lie smooth, and biting them if they appear refractory.' Guinea pigs, Goldsmith concludes, are 'the most timorous creatures upon earth', 'scarce possessed of courage sufficient to defend themselves against the meanest of all quadrupedes, a mouse', and although thoroughly inoffensive, they are 'of very little benefit to mankind. Some, indeed, dress and eat them; but their flesh is indifferent food, and by no means a reward for the trouble of rearing them.' However, he acknowledges that people *do* rear them, 'to satisfy caprice', and includes advice on their care, such as the importance of supplying them with a fresh bed of hay once a week.[11]

Goldsmith's aspersions upon guinea pigs are repeated by the naturalist and wood engraver Thomas Bewick. 'Great numbers', he writes, 'are kept in a domestic state; but for what purpose can hardly be determined. They have neither beauty nor utility to recommend them: their skins are of little value; and their flesh, though eatable, is far from being good.'[12] Isabella Beeton correctly noted that 'Domestication seems to have completely revolutionized the appearance and habits of the Guinea pig. The colours borne by the animal with which we are familiar, are never seen with the wild animals busy with their domestic affairs among the Bromelia Groves of Paraguay.'[13] However, in her famous *Book of Household Management* she was scornful of this caged descendant, considering that its only value lay in keeping rats away from rabbit hutches:

Rats, however, it is said, carefully avoid them; and for this reason they are frequently bred by rabbit-fanciers, by way of protection for their young stock against those troublesome vermin. The lower tier of a rabbit-hutch is esteemed excellent quarters by the guinea-pig; here, as he runs loose, he will devour the waste food of his more admired companion . . . The usual ornament of an animal's hind quarters is denied them; and were it not for this fact, and also for their differences in colour, the Shakespearean locution 'a rat without a tail', would designate them very properly.[14]

The novelist George Eliot, who was a farmer's daughter, was evidently familiar with guinea pigs, for she introduces them into several of her stories. In *Daniel Deronda* (1876) the Jewish pawnbroker Cohen, bargaining with Daniel over the value of a ring, has 'a pair of glistening eyes that suggested a miraculous guinea-pig'; while Mrs Crackenthorp, the rector's wife in *Silas Marner* (1861), is portrayed as 'a small blinking woman, who fidgeted incessantly with her lace, ribbons, and gold chain, turning her head about and making subdued noises, very much like a guinea-pig that twitches its nose and soliloquizes in all company indiscriminately'. Like many other observers then and now, George Eliot was particularly intrigued by the sounds guinea pigs made: Mr Pilgrim, the local doctor in 'The Sad Fortunes of the Reverend Amos Barton', the first of her *Scenes of Clerical Life* (1858), emits 'a succession of little snorts, something like the treble grunts of a guinea-pig, which were always with him the sign of suppressed disapproval'. In all these examples, the humans who are likened to guinea pigs are somehow suppressed within their social milieu, and are unable to express their real identities: Cohen is an outsider by virtue of his Jewishness and Mrs Crackenthorp's feeble maunderings are not treated as proper speech, while the doctor is forced to mute his opinions so as not to annoy the formidable Mrs Hackit, the source of a good proportion of his income.

The second of Eliot's *Scenes of Clerical Life*, 'Mr Gilfil's Love Story', follows the tragic history of the orphaned Italian girl Caterina, who is fostered by Sir Christopher Cheverel and his wife and brought to live at Cheverel Manor. Although her musical talent and wonderful singing voice serve to raise her in the social scale, her position is always anomalous, and becomes unbearable when she falls deeply in love with Anthony, Sir Christopher's nephew and heir. After his death from heart failure, she comes close to losing her reason and, although she makes a partial recovery and marries her devoted admirer Maynard Gilfil, she is so weakened by her agonizing experiences that she too dies young. Maynard, kindly and stable, is contrasted with the irresponsible Anthony, and the security and simple enjoyments of the life he offers are described at the beginning and the end of the story, bookending the disruptive passions that form the substance of

Caterina's tale. Guinea pigs, along with other humble pets such as rabbits and squirrels, reinforce this theme: when the schoolboy Maynard leaves the child Caterina to go back to boarding school, he entrusts them to her care: 'You won't forget me, Tina, before I come back again? I shall leave you all the whip-cord we've made; and don't you let Guinea die. Come, give me a kiss, and promise not to forget me.'

Years later, after the death of Anthony, Caterina draws comfort from the relationship she forms with Oswald ('Ozzy'), Maynard's young nephew:

> With something of his uncle's person, he had inherited also his uncle's early taste for a domestic menagerie, and was very imperative in demanding Tina's sympathy in the welfare of his guinea-pigs, squirrels, and dormice. With him she seemed now and then to have gleams of her childhood coming athwart the leaden clouds, and many hours of winter went by the more easily for being spent in Ozzy's nursery.

Jakob Bogdani, *Capuchin Squirrel Monkey, Two Guinea Pigs, a Blue Tit and an Amazon St Vincent Parrot with Peaches, Figs and Pears in a Landscape*, c. 1710–20.

These 'domestic' guinea pigs suggest a gentle, undemanding round of care, and it is easy to associate them with a picture such as George Morland's *Selling Guinea Pigs*, in which two young girls at a farmhouse door are charmed by the little animals, which creep out of a straw-lined basket. (Eliot sets her story in 1788; Morland's picture was painted only a year or so later.)

The appeal of guinea pigs for small girls and boys was exploited in various ways in nineteenth-century Britain, and we get glimpses of this in the children's literature of the time, which was often of an 'improving' nature. In one of *Mamma's Stories*, published in London in 1843, a shady-looking youth turns up at Anna's house with a guinea pig for sale in a basket. He insists it is full of 'diverting tricks and gambols', which it only fails to demonstrate because of its 'shyness', and poor Anna is torn between this new delight and a doll her mother has promised her. While she havers, her father intervenes and sends the boy away. The guinea pig is palmed off on Anna's cousin Fanny, and predictably it soon sickens and dies. Anna learns the valuable lesson that one should resist an initial impulse to acquire something tempting – in other words, 'think before you shop'.

In 'Jack and his Dancing Guinea Pig', ten-year-old Jack wanders the countryside with his black and white pet, desperately seeking to earn a few pennies by showing off Guinea's ability to 'cut capers on his hind legs'. Jack, an orphan, has run away from his master, the Fagin-like organ grinder Mr Jerry Joker, 'a cruel man, who kept several small boys, and sent them daily out into the streets, one with a monkey, another with white mice, and so on, to pick up a living for themselves and something for him'; he whips them if they come back empty-handed. After a couple of rebuffs, Jack is taken in by old Betty Frost, who warms him at her fire and feeds him and Guinea with a large bowl of bread and milk. The pious Betty detects God's will in the arrival of Jack, who has the same name

George Morland,
Selling Guinea Pigs,
c. 1789.

as her own son, who was lost at sea; Jack is invited to stay, and
he helps Betty with her work as a 'tater woman until upward
mobility beckons and he is offered an apprenticeship to a draper.
Meanwhile Guinea, having lived out his allotted span, is given
'honourable burial under a large apple-tree in the garden'.[15]

There seem to have been troops of 'guinea-pig boys' like
Jack in nineteenth-century cities: one American children's book
includes these plaintive verses, spoken by one of them:

James Ward,
*A Study of
Guinea Pigs,*
1794.

Ah! little master, stay awhile
My guinea-pigs to see;
They're all that I have in the world
To love or care for me.
I've tended them since they were born,
Until they know me well;
And all the tricks that they can do
'Twould take me long to tell.
They'll hunt my pocket or my sleeve
To find a piece of bread;
Jump over sticks, or patient sit,
And wait till they are fed.

I have some young ones in my box,
Marked in a manner rare;
I'll sell them to you cheap enough,
If you would like a pair.
Ah! master, do not turn away,
To me a trifle give;
You do not know how hard it is
For us poor boys to live.[16]

'I'm poor Italian Guinea-pig boy', announces the speaker of a popular song current in the 1860s; 'Straight from Florence I come with my stock',

Ven I leave Italy my friends say, 'good bye,'
We no see you 'gain, but my Guinea cry 'queak,'
I fall in ze water and ze people all stare,
But mine Guinea jump'd in and pull me out by ze hair.

Presumably the daft lyrics gained something from being sung with a cod accent and accompanied with appropriate gestures. On the cover of the music sheets the boy is portrayed with a travelling cage of guinea pigs slung from his shoulders. Despite being accident-prone, he gets lucky in the end:

Vell I recover'd and come here to England,
O it so good I no go back again,
Zo for my troubles I care not von fig,
So that I please with my little Guinea pig.[17]

Many guinea-pig boys were indeed brought over from Italy and 'managed' by the organ grinders whose instruments belted out a cacophony in the crowded city streets (does Jerry Joker's

name suggest garbled Italian?). The guinea pigs were used to attract passing children, who were encouraged to pet them while their parents were no doubt offered some of the surplus stock. However, the player of 'the bones' (pairs of sticks or spoons – another traditional organ grinding accompaniment) whom the journalist James Greenwood meets in the countryside in 1874 complains that, because of new regulations, the trade is nothing like it used to be:

> Do I know of many boys that are brought here by padrones? There used to be a regular swarm of 'em but the magistrates stopped that. You won't find one – either a hurdy-gurdy, or white mice, or guinea-pig boy – where you might one time find twenty. The boys took care of themselves as soon as they found the chance. As soon as they came to know that the magistrate was on their side, it was all over with the padrone ill-using 'em, or getting a living out of 'em for that matter. They're naturally a laying-about, lazy lot of little beggars in their own country, and as soon as they found out that the man that hired 'em and brought 'em over was bound to feed 'em, and daren't wollop 'em, they let him have a nice life of it. He used to be afraid to offend 'em for fear they should put themselves in the way to be locked up and get him fined forty shillin's.[18]

Although the provenance of individual pets might be a trifle dubious, the keeping of guinea pigs had certainly become a popular pastime by the nineteenth century. Beatrix Potter's friend Elizabeth Ann ('Nina') Paget, who was also a near neighbour of hers in Bolton Gardens, South Kensington, owned 'an infinite number of guinea pigs', which implies a large area, perhaps a basement, in which they could all be kept. Nina occasionally

Henry Melville after George Stevens, *Italian Boys, Mischief,* 1847.

65

Mille bien affectueux baisers. Madeleine

Thomas Williams, 'Two Guinea Pigs', from *Every Boy's Book*, c. 1843–62.

lent her pets to Beatrix so she could draw them – once, at least, with a disastrous result:

> *Sunday, February 5th* [1893]. I went to the Pagets somewhat guiltily . . . First I borrowed and drew *Mr Chopps*. I returned him safely. Then in an evil hour I borrowed a very particular guinea-pig with a long white ruff, known as *Queen Elizabeth*. This PIG – offspring of *Titwillow the Second*, descendant of the *Sultan of Zanzibar*, and distantly related to a still more illustrious animal named the *Light of Asia* – this wretched pig took to eating blotting paper, pasteboard, string, and other curious substances, and expired in the night.
>
> I suspected something was wrong and intended to take it back. My feelings may be imagined when I found

A soulful Italian boy begs with his guinea pig, postcard, c. 1900.

Beatrix Potter,
'Guinea pigs in
a basket', from
*Appley Dapply's
Nursery Rhymes*
(1917).

it extended a damp – very damp disagreeable body. Miss
Paget proved peaceable, I gave her the drawing.[19]

Nina evidently constructed family trees for her guinea pigs,
and it is possible that she noted patterns of inheritance of particular characteristics, such as curled hair and coat colour – as
the young Jack and Naomi Haldane were later to do, in a more
avowedly scientific way. In the same diary entry in which she
records the sad fate of Queen Elizabeth, Potter records being
teased about her 'guinea PIG drawings' in 'a pompous but perfectly kind manner' by the Liberal politician and philanthropist
William Rathbone:

He wanted to know whether they were intended for carica-
ture of Mr Paget, thought there was a certain resemblance
– er – about er – the white hair. I said such a suggestion
amounted to contempt of court. He stated elaborately
that it was a compliment. I asked him 'to Mr Paget or the
pig?' and he didn't know.

Many years later, in 1925, Potter wrote to her editor, Fruing
Warne, describing her own guinea pig, Tuppenny:

I have got a white guinea pig . . . he is rather like a rat without a tail, he has the same kind of little pink hands and
feet. He is a very talkative friendly person – only he *won't*
let me touch him. He is in a small rabbit hutch with wire
netting on the bottom and he nibbles the grass off short.
Directly he hears my footsteps he begins to twitter like a
little bird, but if I try to touch him – he rushes about his
box.[20]

Much of the credit for the growing popularity of breeding
guinea pigs as 'a fancy' is due to Charles Cumberland, a Victorian
Fellow of the Zoological Society whose book *Guinea Pigs and
How to Keep Them* appeared in 1896 as one of a series of practical handbooks published by L. Upcott Gill (other volumes
included *Practical Taxidermy, Butterfly and Moth Collecting* and
– perhaps more worryingly – *Firework-Making for Amateurs*).
'Most of us are familiar with the appearance of the animal',
Cumberland writes.[21] This suggests that guinea pigs, although
common, were not yet ubiquitous (an impression possibly re-
inforced by Beatrix Potter's careful description of what Tuppenny
actually looks like). Despite their inroads into urban culture,
Cumberland's characterization of them as 'the cottager's cattle',

and his description of them 'running loose in . . . kitchens . . . in the more rural parts' associates them chiefly with farms and the countryside, where small tribes may have owed their origin to passing pedlars such as the one painted by Morland.[22] Cumberland's task, as he sees it, is to establish them as a 'project' for the respectable hobbyist.

Cumberland's interest in breeding guinea pigs sprang from the recent arrival of two new varieties, the Abyssinian and the Peruvian. When these were crossed with the 'old smooth Cavy' many attractive permutations of coat colour and texture could be produced:

> In some there is a mane along the back; in others, much moustache; in others, again, a tuft on the head; and one peculiar variation I have bred from has a smooth head, with remarkable long pendent hair behind. Then, again, if we mix the colours, and breed to pattern, there could be no end to the possible variations of markings.

Cumberland hoped that a network of 'Cavy clubs' would be established, so that an individual fancier would be able, 'by free exchange of stock, [to] derive some of the advantages possessed by the breeder on a large scale – viz., the power to select promising matches, and to avoid the evil effects of consanguinity'.[23]

On one level, Cumberland treats his guinea pigs solely as instruments: breeding cavies is the democratized equivalent of breeding horses or cattle, affording the same kinds of satisfaction but much more quickly and cheaply. Now members of the middle class could run their own little 'studs' and enlarge their social circles by mingling with other enthusiasts. They could also exercise their practical skills by building hutches and runs, food hoppers and drinking fountains, for all of which Cumberland

The cover of Charles Cumberland's guide to guinea pig keeping.

Guinea Pigs

& How to Keep Them

Price 1/- NETT.

LONDON. L. UPCOTT GILL.

A guinea pig keeper, as envisaged by Cumberland.

provides instructions and diagrams. He gives thought to keeping guinea pigs in small London gardens – perfectly possible, with stacked hutches fronted with curtains 'of stout, cheap linen' that could be drawn at night and in severe weather. However, smelly foods such as swedes or cabbages should be avoided so as not to annoy the neighbours.[24] Cumberland's guinea pigs are cared for scrupulously but they are part of the owner's capital: the best specimens will be bred from, while others – the 'weeds' – will be fattened for the table, a fate Cumberland thought was entirely consonant with his overall aims.

However, there are also glimmers of a warmer attitude. Cumberland's scientific bent led him to weigh his guinea pigs and record the results. The average for full-grown animals was 30 oz (850 g), but a certain 'Bobby', who 'ran loose about a kitchen and was much petted', tipped the scales at 48 oz (1,360 g), the excess, his owner had to admit, being 'due to fat only'. Cumberland's first guinea pig, which he and his sister bought for sixpence, is also fondly remembered: it 'trotted round, and cried "a week, a week," without cessation. It was banished (to our brief misery), because it ate the leather of the kitchen bellows.'[25] The book's final chapter considers 'Cavies as pets', and defends them against the common view that they are stupid:

> I . . . may tell the careful observer, that he will find in these little animals, if he studies them, a fund of intelligence that will well repay him for his trouble; he will learn the meaning of their various cries, and will find that they possess much individuality of character . . . A Cavy will know the voice and footstep of its owner; will greet with joyful cries his return after an occasional absence, and show evident joy upon seeing him again.[26]

Cumberland describes guinea pigs of his acquaintance who refuse to eat bread with no jam on it, or to drink plain water once they have tasted milk, who sup 'a teaspoonful and a half of coffee at breakfast . . . and the same quantity of tea at tea time', who answer to their name, who enjoy a playful friendship with the family cat. As often, special interest attaches to their varied calls: when stroked the wrong way, one produces,

> a sort of whimpering grumble. When he wants anything to eat, he gives a loud, shrill shriek, and then breaks off into

a whimper until he gets what he wants. If the kitchen clock strikes, or the bells ring, he shows his displeasure by giving a peculiar chuckling sound.[27]

These guinea pigs seem to live indoors, and perhaps that is the distinction between them and their farmed relations in the garden; certainly it is disconcerting that Cumberland ends his book by turning abruptly from the antics of little 'Bob' and 'Piggie' to instructions for curing 'Cavy skins' (especially as the results are hardly worth the trouble).

4 On the Menu

Social media sites are scattered with diary accounts, photos and video clips from backpackers and other travellers who have sampled *cuy* in a Peruvian or Ecuadorian restaurant. Comments on these range from the admiring or curious to the frankly horrified. Television presenter Phillip Schofield sparked outrage when he posted a picture on Twitter of what one newspaper described as his 'roasted feral dinner'. Andrew Tyler, director of Animal Aid, commented, 'This callous provocation is despicable.' Schofield, however, argued that he was respecting Peruvian customs, and that the guinea pigs had been humanely farmed, enjoying a 'free range' lifestyle unlike that of the battery chickens we unthinkingly consume. His verdict on his meal was: 'It's very tasty, but the skin is a bit tough.'[1] The science and wildlife presenter Kate Humble shared spit-roasted guinea pigs with her alpaca-herding hosts in the high Andes, and pronounced them 'delicious', like 'dark chicken meat'.[2]

Poet and teacher Lynn Levin ordered *cuy al horno* (oven-roasted guinea pig) in a restaurant called El Candamo in Aguas Calientes, the spa town which is also the gateway to Machu Picchu:

> It cost 32 *soles* or about $10, and I watched with some trepidation as the cook took the small prepared mammal, laid it on a shallow white tray, and slid it into a wood-burning

Guinea pigs brought to market in Ecuador.

clay oven . . . Fluffy lay on the plate congealed and scorched, paws up, claws and head on, ringed with papas fritas, a huge log of *choclo* [maize], and a few slices of cucumber and tomato . . . The body of the *cuy* was pierced at various points to let the fat run out. With much difficulty I split it open with the dull table knife. Inside there was a dark green stuffing, made mostly of parsley and flavored with various herbs. It was potent and aromatic, but as I dipped in a second time, I came up with a fork of noodle-like stuff; the animal's intestines were mixed in with the green . . . I took a deep breath for courage then cut and mostly combed at the meat with my fork. It was a labor-intensive dish. I found I had to separate the thin sheets of meat from the leather and subcutaneous fat . . . It was pungent, perhaps from the herb stuffing. There was a slipperiness to it. It was stringy and chewy and tasted like pork.

Lynn's friend, the poet Odi Gonzales, an ethnic Inca, later explained to her that cutlery isn't needed: you are supposed to pick up the whole *cuy* and suck the meat off the thin bones. Reflecting on her experience, Lynn concluded that there was 'something shocking about the frankness of seeing the cooked body entire'. This was something different from the challenge of sheer strangeness, for, as she points out, 'Rodent eating . . . is not unheard of even in America. Squirrel is a classic ingredient in Brunswick stew. In some parts of New Jersey, fire companies and churches hold muskrat dinners.' Meanwhile, the Peruvians 'think it is bizarre and hilarious that Americans keep guinea pigs as pets'.[3]

Guinea pig prepared in another way features in an episode (first screened on 12 March 2007) of *Bizarre Foods with Andrew Zimmern*, a series in which the American celebrity chef and food writer explores some of the more outré examples of international cuisine. In Quito he visits Fiambre Restaurant, and is first invited to choose his dinner from a pen of scrambling animals. After its dispatch (which we do not see) the guinea pig is skewered and cooked in a coal-fired oven for about 90 minutes, then garnished with avocados and tomatoes and served with a bowl of potatoes. Zimmern correctly eats with his fingers, describing the meat as 'extremely sweet' and like 'roast pork shoulder'. He finds the skin, rubbed with garlic and salt, particularly delicious, and devours the tiny white blob of brain in the way his Ecuadorian friends show him, by sucking it out of the skull.

Two years after Zimmern's exploits were broadcast, the German Association of Lutheran Churches, based in Stuttgart, included a guinea pig recipe in their cookbook entitled *Give Us This Day Our Daily Bread*, which presented flavoursome dishes from around the world. The book advises buying (presumably from a pet shop) a 'good fat guinea pig' weighing at least 1 kg, and first boiling it so that it can be skinned more easily. It should then be baked

A woman examines a guinea pig in Saquisilí market, Ecuador.

Guinea pigs for sale in Saquisilí market, Ecuador.

and served with a chilli sauce and sweet potatoes. Naturally the recipe met with appalled disapproval in many quarters, prompting the UK *Metro* news headline: 'Animal lovers have given church officials a roasting'. Claudia Wehling, from the Stuttgart Guinea Pig Association, declared, 'It is shocking. Eating pets is not part of our culture', while Dr Edmund Haferbach, German spokesperson for the animal rights group PETA (People for the Ethical Treatment of Animals), concurred: 'This is a disgrace – I don't know what the church was thinking of.' The writers of the cookbook defended themselves vigorously: 'Guinea pig is regarded as a nutritious meal in the Andes. It is easily digested and has a lot of good nutritional content', said their representative, Karin Achtelstetter.[4]

However, guinea pig meat has a special status in its Andean homeland: it embodies codes of social interaction and cannot be viewed, say, as just a packet of protein. An additional example of a group consuming it as part of a shared celebratory meal is the barbecue, or *pachamanca* ('earthen pot' in Quechua), of the Peruvian highlands. Here the tasks of building a small, igloo-shaped oven, collecting fuel and preparing and seasoning the guinea pigs are divided between the participants. Once the oven is red hot, its stones are raked apart and the meat is laid on them:

> After the meat is seasoned with fresh aromatic herbs, two or three clean, empty woolen sacks or large paper bags are placed on top of it. Finally a layer of dirt is shoveled on top to make a small mound . . . After about one hour, the layers of insulation are removed and the food picked up on trays, dishes, or corn husks.[5]

In the later part of the twentieth century the Peruvian government initiated programmes promoting the commercial rearing of guinea pigs. This was seen as a way for small farmers to raise themselves out of poverty. In the 1970s, for example, researchers at the National Agrarian University of La Molina collected guinea pigs from all over Peru and gathered data on their husbandry. They discovered that farmers typically ate or sold the largest and fattest animals, leaving the smaller ones to breed; they were thus inadvertently reducing the average size of the population. The staff of La Molina then began an experimental breeding programme using only the largest and best-conditioned guinea pigs. The programme was spectacularly successful, and they were soon able to start exporting the 'Peruvian Breed', which are fast-growing, tastier and weigh up to 3 kg (guinea pigs raised in typical rural households rarely exceed 800–900 g). Through a far-seeing government initiative, every time a farmer ate an unimproved male guinea pig, he or she received a fresh animal from the new giant stock, so that the genes for large size and quick growth could be disseminated as effectively as possible.[6]

The breeding programme was intended to help poor families increase their income by raising animals for the overseas market. In 2005, lecturers from La Molina ran a three-month course in Huarmey, a coastal region about 250 km north of Lima, for 80

Women roast guinea pigs during the *Fiesta de Toros* in Girón, Ecuador.

A Peruvian woman holds one of her guinea pigs.

Flowers may be fed to guinea pigs to enhance the flavour of the meat.

local women, educating them in scientifically proven husbandry techniques. As Gloria Palacios, director of the university's small livestock farm, observed, 'Even the poorest family can afford to raise guinea pigs.' Each participant received eight starter guinea pigs – one male and seven females. The success of the project is illustrated by the story of Rosa Casimiro, a single mother who also supported her parents from the produce of a small 5-acre farm. By 2009 she had more than 200 animals and was able to market 70 each month, earning about $300 in sales, more than double her previous income. She also became the president of her locally formed Small Livestock Breeders Association.[7]

Today there are many commercial guinea pig farmers, in Peru and Ecuador, and stock numbers of more than 2,000 are not uncommon. A supply chain has been established, with exporters buying the live animals directly from farms, slaughtering them in their small plants, packing the meat in well-sealed plastic bags and shipping it out of the continent. However, there is also a strong local market. One farmer in northern Ecuador has more than 40,000 guinea pigs on his two farms. He slaughters about 500 a day for local consumption, and does not bother dealing with exporters because his business is already extremely profitable – in fact he cannot keep up with the demand.[8] In addition, with the increase in tourism, more guinea pigs are served in restaurants throughout the Andean countries, and chefs have capitalized on the curiosity of tourists who wish to try 'authentic' native cuisine (one researcher was amused to find 'guinea-pig cooked in bread-crumbs, a kind of "Wiener schnitzel" guinea-pig', on the menu of a tavern in Quito).[9]

Exported guinea pig meat has found a ready market in expatriate Peruvian and Ecuadorian communities in countries such as Japan and the United States. Urubamba, a Peruvian restaurant in Queens, New York, offers *cuy* one weekend every month. 'The animals go for $17 a plate, each *cuy* splayed down the middle like a lobster and served with a front leg and a back, an eye, an ear and a nostril.'[10] One entrepreneur even offered canned guinea pig in a choice of sauces (red, peanut or *pachamanca*) and succeeded in selling a shipment to Spanish consumers. However, traders have had to contend with the animal's signature identity as a pet in many cultures. In the UK the British Cavy Council campaigned against the import of meat from the new, larger, specially bred animals, arguing that such was the guinea pig's popularity in Britain that eating it would be just as unacceptable as eating a dog or a cat.

Advocates point out that guinea pig is tasty, high in protein and low in fat and cholesterol. The animals are also easy to keep and cause little damage to their environment. In Colombia, where the clearing of forests to provide cattle pasture has caused erosion and water pollution, conservation groups are encouraging farmers to switch to guinea pig farming as a greener alternative. The humanitarian organization Heifer International now includes guinea pigs among the 'starter' animals it distributes to families

Cuy festival in Santa Cruz, Peru.

A guinea pig keeper in the North Kivu province of DR Congo.

in Peru who had previously relied on the more precarious coffee bean harvest. Their spokesman, Jason Woods, points out that, pound for pound, guinea pigs are twice as efficient as cows at turning their feed into meat.[11] Guinea pig farming has also become popular in a number of African countries, including Nigeria, Cameroon, Ghana, Sierra Leone, Togo and Zaire, and in the Philippines, where the animals are raised in small cages or even cardboard boxes.[12]

Indeed, if we had followed the recommendations of Charles Cumberland, we would all be eating farmed guinea pigs in Britain today. As part of his enthusiastic advocacy of the guinea pig 'fancy', Cumberland proposed a thriving trade in 'weeds' – animals that were superfluous to the breeder's requirements. That they should

A guinea pig farm in Ecuador.

be sold for the table presented him with no dilemma: it was, he thought, simply putting the creature 'to the use for which it was primarily domesticated – that is, make food of it'.[13] Cumberland helpfully supplies several recipes, from a prosaic 'Brown Soup' to the more exotic Cavy Curry and Cavy aux Fines Herbes. 'Think of . . . the value of its tender flesh and gelatinous skin in the feeding of invalids and convalescents', he pleads; 'For invalids it admirably replaces those stewed calves' feet which doctors are so fond of ordering, and which, in country places, are often so difficult to procure.'[14] While acknowledging his fellow countrymen's deep-rooted reluctance to sample any new food, Cumberland remained irrepressibly optimistic:

> The number of people who are willing to try the gastronomic experience of 'Cavy' increases daily, and I have now sanguine hopes that the principal object I had in view when I began the cultivation of the Cavy is in a fair way of accomplishment . . . I have little doubt that, before long, no poultry show will be complete without classes for Cavies, and I have good reason to hope that, at a time not too far distant, Cavy, in some of its savoury and delicious preparations, will be considered a requisite in a good *menu*.[15]

Cumberland was not the first British gourmand to sample guinea pig, for we saw that Oliver Goldsmith, in the late eighteenth century, observed that some of his contemporaries had tried them. Isabella Beeton gives the topic a passing mention; however, she, like Goldsmith, is uncomplimentary. 'Their flesh,' she concludes, 'although eatable, is decidedly unfit for food; they have been tasted, however, we presume by some enthusiast eager to advance the cause of science, or by some eccentric epicure in search of new pleasure for his palate.'[16]

Finally, Professors Carmen Felipe-Morales and Ulises Moreno, of La Molina, Peru, have taken a further step in guinea pig husbandry and employ their vast herd to generate electricity. The animals, which are fed a nutritionally enriched diet, excrete about 3 tonnes of droppings every month. Most of this is turned into organic compost, but about 200 kg are fed into a bio-digester to which water is added, and bacteria to metabolize the slurry: the products are methane gas and a dark-brown liquid plant nutrient, which the professors use to increase the yield of their fruit orchard. The methane is ingeniously stored in a collection of large rubber inner tubes, and provides more than sufficient energy to power all the family's electrical devices.[17]

5 Experimental Subjects

The Chambers Dictionary gives as the secondary meaning of 'guinea-pig': 'a person used as the subject of an experiment (as the cavy commonly is in the laboratory)'. We use the expression in a wide variety of contexts, probably with a vague acceptance of the bracketed phrase at the back of our minds: if guinea pigs are not in hutches in our gardens, then, we assume, they are in the hands of scientists somewhere. The *Oxford English Dictionary* agrees: a guinea pig is a 'S. Amer. rodent of genus *Cavia*, kept as pet or for research in biology'. It may be a surprise, therefore, to learn that they now make up only a small fraction – perhaps 2 per cent – of the total population of experimental animals, far less numerous than rats or mice, for example. However, historically guinea pigs have made an enormous contribution to biological research: Jim Endersby, in his excellent study of their role, estimates that they have helped in the winning of 23 Nobel Prizes.[1] These include the prizes for Physiology or Medicine awarded to Charles Nicolle for his work on typhus (1928), and to Selman A. Waksman for his discovery of streptomycin, the first antibiotic effective against TB (1952).

Small, docile, easy to handle and to rear, guinea pigs were historically the subjects of choice, while rats and mice, by contrast, were shunned because of their popular association with infection and disease (in the first decade of the twentieth century,

Elmer V. McCollum, who discovered the importance of vitamins in a healthy diet, and after whom the laboratory strain of 'McCollum rats' is named, was told by the dean of the Agricultural College at the University of Wisconsin that he would be disgraced if he was found to be using 'federal and state funds to feed rats').[2] This chapter is necessarily selective, focusing on just a handful of scientific projects involving guinea pigs, and on the debates that their treatment has provoked.

Guinea pigs began their long career as scientific subjects in the seventeenth century, when the Italian biologists Marcello Malpighi and Carlo Fracassati dissected live specimens, injecting coloured water into their lungs and the associated blood vessels in order to reveal the organ's microstructure. Fortunately for the guinea pigs, the technique proved too difficult and the scientists moved on to frogs instead.[3] The English physician William Harvey, who discovered the circulation of the blood, numbered guinea pigs among his subjects when he investigated how the placenta was attached to the wall of the womb in different animals.[4]

In the 1780s the pioneering French chemist Antoine Lavoisier treated guinea pigs somewhat more humanely in his attempts to measure the amount of heat produced during respiration. He placed one of the animals in the central chamber of a calorimeter, encircled by an inner shell filled with ice. The outer shell of the device was packed with snow, which melted to maintain a constant temperature of 0°C. The melting of the ice in the inner shell was thus the result of the guinea pig's breathing as it drew in oxygen and exhaled carbon dioxide. Lavoisier collected and weighed the water which flowed out of the calorimeter, and was thus able to estimate the heat generated by the guinea pig's metabolism. He concluded that respiratory gas exchange is a combustion, comparing it to a candle burning.

Meanwhile the dissection of live and dead animals continued as scientists attempted to map the body and its functions. The general view was that animals, lacking reason and immortal souls, were inferior to humans and had been put on the earth to benefit us, so their instrumental use was justified. While few were as thoroughgoing as the Jansenists of the Paris monastery of Port-Royal, who denied that beasts could feel pain at all, and claimed that the cries emitted by the dogs they experimented on were merely 'the noise of a little spring which had been touched',[5] the notion that it was intrinsically wrong to make animals suffer was slow to develop. The English naturalist and clergyman John Ray was ahead of his time when he declared that 'the torture of animals is no part of philosophy.'[6]

However, by the middle of the nineteenth century, concern about the welfare of animals, and disquiet at some of the activities of scientists, had become matters of public debate. In 1822 the British Parliament had passed an Act forbidding cruelty to farm animals (later amended to include cats and dogs). Popular fervour was frequently stirred by accounts of atrocities perpetrated by foreign scientists such as François Magendie, who allegedly nailed 'a lady's greyhound' to a table, or the French veterinarians at the school at Alfort, who performed operations on unanaesthetized horses as part of their training.[7] The driving force of the opposition to vivisection in Britain was Frances Power Cobbe, who in 1875 persuaded the government to set up a Royal Commission to investigate the practice; in the same year she founded the Victoria Street Society for the Protection of Animals from Vivisection, whose supporters included the poets Alfred, Lord Tennyson, and Robert Browning. The outcome of the work of the Royal Commission was the Cruelty to Animals Act of 1876 (which remained in force in Britain until 1986). It required scientists working on animals to apply for licences from the Home Office, although since such licences proved easy to obtain the Act did little to reduce the incidence of experimentation.

One argument used by anti-vivisectionists was that the majority of experiments on animals added nothing to the sum of human knowledge. The Mauritius-born physiologist Charles-Édouard Brown-Séquard came in for particular obloquy. His attempts to prove that damage to the nerves of the spinal cord produced epileptic symptoms involved severing the sciatic nerve in guinea pigs and observing the loss of motor control which resulted. His methods provoked a lively debate in *Scribner's Monthly*, with one correspondent pointedly appealing to the animal's intrinsic charm and innocence: 'about the size of a half-grown kitten', the guinea pig emitted 'piercing little squeaks' as it 'ran in desperate circles' after the inflicted injury. 'This experiment had not the slightest relation whatever to the cure of disease', the writer concluded. Others, though, came to Brown-Séquard's defence, citing particular examples of patients who had been cured of epilepsy by the application of his methods.[8] Charles Darwin was interested in the evidence the experiments provided for his theories of inheritance; he took it on trust from Brown-Séquard that the offspring of the animals operated on also developed epilepsy in due course, and concluded: 'On the whole, we can hardly avoid admitting, that injuries and mutilations, especially when followed by disease, or perhaps exclusively when thus followed, are occasionally inherited.'[9]

The advances of microbiology, pioneered by scientists such as Louis Pasteur, Émile Roux and Robert Koch, tended to undercut the anti-vivisectionists' arguments about needless suffering, for the discovery that many life-threatening diseases were transmitted by microscopic infectious agents appeared to offer the possibility that cures could be found. Guinea pigs played a vital role in research into germ theory in the later nineteenth and early twentieth centuries.

In 1877 the German physician Robert Koch succeeded in cultivating the anthrax bacterium – a rod-shaped microbe that had been observed in the blood of victims – in the aqueous humour of an ox's eye. Koch believed that each different microbe was exclusively associated with a particular disease; the challenge for the scientist was therefore to isolate the microorganism, grow it in a sterile environment and then prove that it indeed induces the disease by injecting the culture into a healthy animal. He developed techniques for staining slides that enabled bacteria far smaller than the relatively large anthrax rods to be examined under the microscope, and, now funded by the German government and helped by a number of co-workers, succeeded in identifying the tuberculosis bacillus in 1882 and the cholera bacillus in 1883. Guinea pigs were his preferred subjects, and were used both to demonstrate the onset of a disease after inoculation, and recovery after the appropriate antitoxin had been administered.[10] He also showed that the bacilli are airborne by

Guinea pigs are among the participants in this anti-vivisection poster, 'The Revenge of the Animals', 1909.

A stamp from Gabon honours Robert Koch and his guinea pigs.

pumping a spray through a pair of bellows into a pen in his garden containing guinea pigs, mice and rabbits – the animals duly sickened and died.

Koch was particularly eager to develop a vaccine for tuberculosis, which killed almost a seventh of the German population in his time, and he seemed to have the ideal animals for experimentation, since guinea pigs are highly susceptible to TB (even today they are sometimes used to test for its presence in patients). In 1890 he announced that he had discovered a substance called 'tuberculin', which would halt the disease. Unfortunately he was found to have misrepresented his results – he was not able to produce the guinea pigs he said he had cured – and tuberculin, prepared from cultures of tuberculosis bacilli, turned out to be not only ineffective but potentially harmful.

Nevertheless, Koch had shown that microbiology had the potential to supply powerful weapons in the war against life-threatening diseases. A particular success was the development of a vaccine for diphtheria by Emil Behring in 1913, following Theobald Smith's experiments with guinea pigs using a mixture of toxin and antitoxin. The Schick test for diphtheria antibodies was also invented in 1913 (by the Hungarian-born paediatrician Béla Schick), so the New York City public health department was able to start a programme of testing schoolchildren and immunizing those who tested positive. During the 1920s there was a huge drop in cases of the disease, which had previously been a killer, particularly among the young.

Anti-vivisectionists found it harder to make headway once the benefits of microbiological research became apparent. The testing of animals such as guinea pigs by injecting them with toxins and antitoxins was not as grossly invasive as cutting them open; nevertheless, a great amount of suffering was still caused. In addition the numbers of experimental animals multiplied, for countless procedures were needed to verify results and then to calibrate the most effective dosages.

In 1926 Paul de Kruif published his immensely popular book *Microbe Hunters*, which presented the scientists' quest as a series of thrilling adventures related in effervescent prose (one chapter is headed 'Koch: The Death Fighter'). Hollywood took up the 'scientist as hero' theme with films such as *The Story of Louis Pasteur* (1936) and *Dr Ehrlich's Magic Bullet* (1940), with Edward G. Robinson in the title role. De Kruif's scientists are starkly portrayed as the destroyers of vast numbers of guinea pigs and other animals, but paradoxically, such deeds are viewed as an aspect of their superhuman personas: just as they relinquish sleep, food and normal human relationships in their frenzied search for solutions, so they do not hesitate to step across the moral boundaries that restrain the rest of us. 'He became a murderer in his heart, this Emile Roux, and in his head as he came down to the laboratory each morning were half-made wishes for the death of his beasts'; while Emil Behring, in his attempts to find a cure for diphtheria, presides over a 'slaughter-house of dead and dying guinea-pigs' and 'hecatombs of corpses'.[11]

An awareness of the ethical questions involved in animal experimentation appears in Sinclair Lewis's novel *Arrowsmith* (1925). The novel aimed to show a true picture of the career of an American doctor – the Martin Arrowsmith of the title – during the era of microbial discoveries, and Lewis collaborated with Paul de Kruif to ensure the accuracy of his portrayal. In one scene Professor Max Gottlieb (a fictional character who is supposed to have studied with Robert Koch) demonstrates the lethality of the anthrax germ to his bacteriology class:

> The assistant held the guinea pig close; Gottlieb pinched up the skin of the belly and punctured it with a quick downthrust of the hypodermic needle. The pig gave a little jerk, a squeak, and the co-eds shuddered . . . He said quietly, 'This poor animal will now soon be as dead as Moses.'[12]

This guinea pig is not an anonymous 'number': its death incites unease and sympathy. Gottlieb himself compares the lively little creature to one of his duller students: 'Why should I murder him to teach *Dummköpfe*? It would be better to experiment on that fat young man.' Questions like these have not gone away.

One of the great success stories in which guinea pigs have been involved was the discovery of a cure for scurvy. For centuries this disease had afflicted sailors on long sea voyages for trade or exploration, and in the 1870s there was a baffling outbreak in London among young children. There were various theories about what caused scurvy: many linked it to a diet deficient in fresh fruit and vegetables, but others pointed out that daily rations of lime juice on board the polar exploration vessel *Alert* in 1875 had not prevented many of the crew from developing scurvy, and suggested that ptomaine poisoning from bad meat, or infection by lice, might be to blame instead. The Norwegian scientists Axel

Holst and Theodor Frølich were the first to show that diet was certainly implicated. In a paper published in 1907 they described feeding 65 guinea pigs a diet consisting of just a single kind of grain, either whole or milled and baked into bread. All of these animals lost weight and died, and post-mortems revealed that their bones and cartilage had undergone the changes characteristic of scurvy. By contrast, guinea pigs fed a variety of grains supplemented with fresh cabbage, lemon juice and apples remained free of the disease.

The link between scurvy and diet might, in fact, have been discovered much earlier if a finding of the u.s. Department of Agriculture's Bureau of Animal Industry had been properly publicized. The Bureau had been using guinea pigs for research into bacterial diseases in pigs, and in 1895–6 it reported on the death of one of its experimental subjects, 'No. 254':

> When guinea pigs are fed with cereals (bran and oats mixed), without any grass, clover, or succulent vegetables, such as cabbage, a peculiar disease . . . carries them off in from four to eight weeks. The death of No. 254 was undoubtedly due to the absence of such food, as the attendant had neglected to provide it after the disappearance of grass in the fall of the year.[13]

Much more work was needed before the 'antiscorbutic factor' was finally isolated, and named vitamin C. Guinea pigs were consistently used for testing – for example, during the First World War, a research group at the Lister Institute in London led by Dr Harriette Chick, found that if the animals drank a significant amount of raw, untreated milk every day, they were protected against scurvy. Elmer McCollum had previously rejected this theory, but Chick showed that his results had been vitiated by a failure to ascertain that the guinea pigs really had taken their dose – they would refuse to drink the milk if it tasted even slightly sour. McCollum had also been led into error by his experiments with rats, which failed to develop scurvy even when they were fed the same diet which produced it in guinea pigs. He concluded that the guinea pigs' malady was caused by 'intestinal autointoxication' – in other words, they were chronically constipated, and the absorption of bacterial products through the walls of the caecum had a toxic effect. We now know that guinea pigs, like humans – but unlike rats and most other animals – cannot metabolize their own vitamin C: it needs to be included in their diet. We also know that its presence in different fruits and vegetables varies considerably – West Indian sour limes contained far less than Mediterranean sweet limes: hence the problems caused when the British Navy substituted the former for the latter – and that it can be destroyed by some methods of processing or heat treatment (the London infants had been exclusively fed proprietary foods, including condensed milk: when they were given fresh, raw milk they quickly recovered). The discovery of vitamin C and its role in well-being has certainly been of immense benefit to humans, and guinea pigs have played a key part in the story.

The u.s. Bureau of Animal Industry, established in 1862 by Abraham Lincoln, lost out on its chance to prove that scurvy was caused by dietary deficiencies. However, the vast amount of data it collected in the course of its research on guinea pigs did not go to waste, and was vital to the development of the new science of genetics. From using the animals to test vaccines, by the early years of the twentieth century the bureau had progressed to breeding them and recording the results in the form of a catalogue of rubber-stamped guinea pig outlines, each carefully hand-coloured to show the outcome of a particular mating.[14] The bureau's interest was in the effects of inbreeding on farm animals

– and a herd of guinea pigs was much cheaper and easier to maintain than a herd of cows or horses.

The enormous amount of information contained in the guinea pig stamps was analysed by Sewall Wright, one of the pioneers in the mathematical approach to genetic inheritance, who had been seconded to the bureau by his mentor, William E. Castle, in 1915. When Wright moved to a teaching post at the University of Chicago, his families of guinea pigs came with him and were housed in 120 specially built pens. He sometimes brought a guinea pig into his lectures to illustrate the practical playing-out of inheritance in its coat colour, and once (so the story goes) absent-mindedly used one to wipe calculations off a blackboard.[15] Wright discovered that the prolonged inbreeding of lines of guinea pigs brought out traits that had previously been extremely rare, since they were carried by recessive genes and so needed a copy from each parent. Most of these traits were harmful or life-limiting, but a few were useful, and these could be retained in the population by cross-breeding two different lines. The resultant offspring would keep the desired trait but would be healthy (an effect known as hybrid vigour).

William Castle also maintained a very large population of guinea pigs in his Harvard research facility. Like Wright, he was interested in Mendelian theory and in the possibility of creating a new species by planned breeding. In 1911 he travelled to Arequipa, Peru, to collect wild and domesticated cavies for his breeding programme; his first view was of the 'common spotted black-and-white sort familiar to lovers of pet-stock throughout the world', which ran about in the adobe cabins where the natives lived. He also observed a few 'rosetted' examples, plainly related to the 'Abyssinian' variety, which had become popular among American and European fanciers. Wild cavies (*C. cutleri*) were harder to obtain, but he succeeded in collecting a number

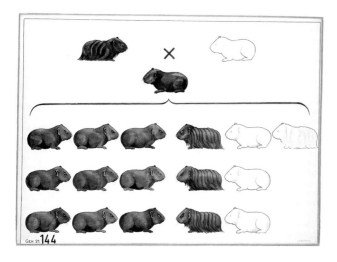

Vintage educational poster illustrating Mendelian genetics.

of live individuals and skins by offering rewards to the local boys. One of the domesticated cavies, 'O 1002', a young 'sepia-cream agouti with white and cream spots', proved to be 'an animal of great vigor and vitality'; shipped back to Harvard, he survived the rigours of the New England climate to sire 'several hundred' sons and daughters and become the undisputed *padre* of the 'Arequipa race'. He was still going strong in 1915 when Castle was writing up his account of the research to which he had made such an important contribution.[16]

For the great modern evolutionary biologist J.B.S. ('Jack') Haldane (1892–1964), the guinea pigs kept by his sister Naomi (the novelist Naomi Mitchison) were the inspiration for his early interest in genetics. As she explained:

Our first joint scientific experiments began when I was about twelve. I had by that time a number of guinea pigs and was making my own observations on their lives and

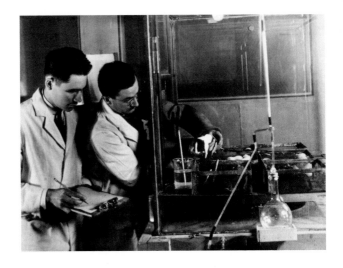

Scientists place a guinea pig in apparatus for a ketone vapour test, c. 1938.

loves. I could separate and mimic, so that they would answer back, at least a dozen calls and cries; I was on intimate terms with them; I knew them as individuals. Once I got one of them to nibble off a wart on my finger, which never returned. Then came Mendelism . . .[17]

Jack and Naomi started to breed their pets systematically, arranging 'marriages, which sometimes went against the apparent inclinations of the partners'. After a while they noticed some puzzling patterns of inheritance in the guinea pig families and were on the verge of making an important discovery about linkage (the tendency of genes that are next to each other on the chromosome to be inherited together) when disaster struck: while Jack was away at Eton, a fox terrier belonging to one of his friends broke into the garden and frightened all the guinea pigs to death by jumping on their cages. The discovery of linkage in mammals therefore had to wait a few more years, until 1912, and Haldane's evidence was eventually drawn not from guinea pigs but from mice.[18]

Today guinea pigs are still widely used as experimental subjects (although, as mentioned above, they comprise only a small fraction of the total lab population), partly because of the ease with which they can be kept and partly because aspects of their physiognomy fit them for particular investigations. For instance, female guinea pigs are prone to toxaemia in pregnancy so can be used to investigate ways of preventing pre-eclampsia in expectant mothers. Guinea pigs, like humans, suffer from arthritis, and a currently running research project at Bristol University reports that when the affected animals are given omega-3 fatty acid (naturally found in fish oils, among other sources) they show a 50 per cent improvement.

Such research may prove to be of great benefit to humans; far less easy to justify is the use of guinea pigs (along with rabbits

Chicks and guinea pigs are examined for signs of nutritional deficiency, 1953.

A poster supporting
the use of animals
in research.

and other animals) to assess the safety of cosmetics, often through painful procedures such as skin patch tests or the application of chemicals to the sensitive lining of the eye. The use of animals for cosmetics testing was banned in the UK in 1998, and in 2004 for cosmetic products and 2008 for cosmetic ingredients in the European Union. In March 2013, thanks in part to the efforts of Tonio Borg, the European Commissioner for Health and Consumer Policy, this *testing* ban was complemented by a *marketing* ban: it is now illegal in all the member states to market any personal care products containing ingredients that have been tested on animals. It is to be hoped that other countries such as the USA and Japan, which at the time of writing still permit this testing, will follow suit.

A statue in Riems, near Munich, commemorates guinea pigs' role in medical research.

Organizations such as Uncaged (soon to become the Centre for Animals and Social Justice) campaign for an end to all animal experimentation, and log the policies of individual companies on their databases. There are also a number of necessarily shadowy groups which engage in direct action against the experimenters. The involvement of one of these cells in a campaign to close down a breeding farm in Newchurch, Staffordshire, became notorious because of the bizarre tactics that were employed.

The campaign to Save the Newchurch Guinea Pigs began in 1999, when members of the Animal Liberation Front raided premises where guinea pigs were being bred before being sold on for research. The ALF removed several hundred animals, but

The logo of OpenMx, a data modelling and statistical analysis toolkit, which was first used to examine the influences of heredity and environment on guinea pig markings.

A u.s. vet checks the pulmonary health of a guinea pig while carrying out research into outbreaks of leptospirosis in Nicaragua.

also shot a video which showed distressing conditions inside the breeding sheds, with many ill or apparently dying guinea pigs lying untended. Roadside demonstrations followed, and hate mail and threats were directed against the Hall family, who owned and ran the farm. In October 2004 the remains of Christopher Hall's mother-in-law were dug up from a churchyard in nearby Yoxall and hidden for well over a year (they were eventually recovered by the police from woodland near Hednesford, following a tip-off). Several animal liberation groups, including Save the Newchurch Guinea Pigs, condemned the deed. Responsibility was claimed, in letters to the BBC and a local newspaper, by a group calling itself the Animal Rights Militia. In May 2006 four activists were convicted of conspiracy to blackmail, and imprisoned. It could not be proved that they had been involved in the original grave robbery, but they admitted they had used it to put pressure on the family. By this time the Halls had given in to the unrelenting pressure upon them and closed their business.

It is worth noting too that guinea pigs have been involved in space research. One was aboard *Sputnik* 9 when it was launched in March 1961. It and its passengers – a dog called Chernushka and several mice – were recovered successfully upon landing. The guinea pigs aboard a biosatellite launched by China in 1990 also survived to tell their tale.

Finally, one of the strangest products of research involving guinea pigs was an almost completely hairless variety, a spontaneous genetic mutation in a breeding colony at Montreal's Institut Armand-Frappier in 1978. A strain of these animals, which are otherwise normal, with a functioning immune system, is used in dermatological research but, more oddly, 'Skinny pigs', as they are called, have become popular pets with their own community of fanciers. A separate mutation, this time in a

A Skinny pig.

breeder's stock, produced the 'Baldwin', which is even balder than the 'Skinny', although it may have minimal hair on its feet. Its foreparts are wrinkly, it has dangly ears and it feels rubbery when touched. There is also a patchily haired 'Werewolf' variety. Contrary to newspaper reports, these recherché little companions do not demand 'factor 50 suncream in the summer and a jumper in the winter' – just warm homes and extra food to maintain their body temperature.[19]

6 Pets, Plain and Fancy

Guinea pigs have been kept as companion animals for several centuries, and as indoor stock, sharing the warmth of the family hearth, for even longer. However, their popularity as pets greatly increased after the Second World War, together with the growth of suburbia and the laying out of generously sized back gardens that could accommodate hutches and runs. Now they are a staple of the pet trade, and a myriad of books provide instructions on their care. It is not hard to uncover the reasons why they are favourites: *gentle, cute, peaceful, cuddly* and *friendly* are frequently applied adjectives, while aficionados also point to their ideal size (ideal, that is, for handling by children), ease of capture (compared to, say, hamsters), and their appealing vocal repertoire (which includes joyful 'wheeps' as soon as food appears).

In the nineteenth century, guinea pigs were often described as 'inoffensive', and this back-handed compliment sometimes accompanied various inaccurate and prejudicial statements. A penny pamphlet on 'How to Manage Rabbits' includes an inserted couple of pages on the guinea pig, in which the writer declares that 'it seems incapable of feeling attachment for those who feed and caress it; even for its own offspring it evinces little affection; it not only suffers them to be destroyed before its face, without making the smallest efforts to defend them, but will even destroy them itself.'[1] Among pets in general, guinea pigs came pretty low down in the hierarchy, exemplified, as we have seen, by their frequent caging underneath the hutches of rabbits to keep the rats away. They were also housed in pigeon lofts, again as rat deterrents: 'They are allowed to run loose about the place and to shift for themselves; the refuse scattered on the floor being sufficient for their subsistence.'[2] Such lack of appropriate care could well be the cause of the stress-related behaviour the author has just described. It also ties in with Charles Cumberland's observation of mass populations kept by breeders: 'I have been informed that the London market is largely supplied from cellars, where the stock are allowed to run about, upon the principle of the "survival of the fittest".'[3]

Since guinea pigs were still seen as faintly exotic, they often found a place in the private menageries owned and managed by gentlemen of leisure. Sir Robert Heron, who also kept kangaroos, coypus and jerboas on his Lincolnshire estate, decided to allow a number of his guinea pigs to run loose throughout the

Child handling a guinea pig at a farm park.

Guinea pig quarters at London Zoo, 1962.

winter; although he had been warned that this was not advisable, he found that his animals remained 'well and lively'. Sadly, though, in 1833 he lost several to a fierce August thunderstorm, against which they were unprotected.[4] Cumberland relates an intriguing rumour: that on the steep slopes of Windsor Castle, 'Guinea Pigs ran wild in considerable numbers, and had to be kept down by ferrets and other means.'[5]

Of course, many individual guinea pigs were much cherished by their owners – Cumberland's own Bobby is a case in point – and even those kept in large gatherings may have been well cared for. However, it is during the twentieth century that the notion of the guinea pig as a gentle and characterful playmate for children really emerges. 'There is an indescribable quaintness about a guinea-pig which makes him very attractive and interesting', Wellesley Pain writes in his *Rabbits: Guinea-pigs: Fancy Mice*, published in 1938 in Blackie's Pets for Young People series. Pain comments on the changed appearance of guinea pigs within his own lifetime:

> The guinea-pigs I saw when I was a boy were not very
> attractive; if you can imagine what a rat would look like
> without his tail you will get a good idea of a guinea-pig's
> appearance in my young days.
>
> The guinea-pig of today is a much nicer animal – better
> in every way – bigger, more symmetrical, more varied in its
> colouring.[6]

This is a reminder of the fact that guinea pigs are an engineered
species and that, since their reproduction is largely controlled
by humans, their bodies will, over time, take on whatever aspects
humans prefer. Although historic pictures of guinea pigs show
animals that look similar to modern ones, there must have been
some that had kept the leaner profile of their wild ancestors.
Both Isabella Beeton and Beatrix Potter likened guinea pigs to
tailless rats. And Cumberland thought that the Abyssinian – an
exciting new breed in his day – had 'a fierce and furtive expression, which reminds us somewhat of the physiognomy of the
rat'. 'This simile', he went on to say, 'is, I think, justified by facts,
as the Abyssinian Cavy is frequently a bold fighter, and more

disposed to combativeness than the old kind'.[7] By 'the old kind' he meant the familiar smooth-haired guinea pig, which he labelled with proprietary pride as 'the English'. Selective breeding has now removed any rattiness, although there are echoes of this primal defect in the language of the cavy 'fancy' (breeding and showing): a prize-winning guinea pig is 'cobby' (chunky) and certainly not 'snipey' – that is, with a long pointed nose, like a snipe's bill.

Pain encouraged his young readers to handle their guinea pigs frequently. He gave sensitive advice about the best way to pick them up and recommended talking to them softly while stroking them with one finger. Once they are accustomed to this they can be groomed with a silk handkerchief (or with a toothbrush if they are rosetted Abyssinians). Such practices would naturally strengthen the bond between the pet and its owner, and modern manuals too place much emphasis on handling and grooming.

Later in the twentieth century the baton of guinea pig advocacy was taken up by Peter Gurney, a bus and lorry driver who retired from his job after injury to devote himself full time to campaigning for the welfare of his pets (he eventually owned about 70 guinea pigs, and remarked on the happy coincidence that his initials were the reverse of theirs). Gurney wrote several books about guinea

One of Charles Cumberland's 'fierce and furtive' Abyssinians, 1896.

A modern
Abyssinian
guinea pig.

pig care, and generously dispensed free advice both over the phone and through his website, which has been kept running in his memory since he died in 2006.[8] Gurney's books show a practical and compassionate approach, finely attuned to the instincts and feelings of his subjects. He had a particular interest in guinea pig healthcare and, since he considered that many vets lacked the necessary expertise, developed a range of simple treatments and remedies, which, again, he was more than willing to share with his fellow pet owners.[9] Michael Bond's Olga (the model for his guinea pig heroine Olga da Polga) was among the animals he treated successfully. It is fair to say that Gurney was a combative and outspoken person, and the Royal College of Veterinary Surgeons, the RSPCA, mindless bureaucrats and anyone involved in hunting and shooting wild creatures (from members of the royal family downwards) were all in his line of fire at one time or another. Nevertheless, guinea pigs could not have wished for a more valiant and devoted champion.

In 1990 it occurred to Gurney that children in hospital might enjoy meeting and interacting with his guinea pigs. He contacted doctors at Great Ormond Street Hospital, who welcomed the idea. Consequently, for several years afterwards,

> Gurney would arrive by Underground pulling a long, narrow plywood box on wheels with wire mesh down one side; inside would be five guinea pigs. He would place an animal on a child's lap and talk about what interested him most – guinea pigs.[10]

This arrangement continued happily until the dreaded bureaucrats put a stop to it, ostensibly for health and safety reasons. Gurney was understandably angry and upset, pointing out that guinea pigs are about the least likely carriers of zoonoses (any diseases that can be passed from animals to humans). A mild fungal skin condition was the only possible risk, and he safeguarded against this by scrupulously checking each of his animals on the morning of a visit.

THE RIGHT SHAPE
Shape in a self. Note the high shoulders,
large eyes—well apart. Drooping ears.

THE WRONG SHAPE
No depth in shoulders. Small upstanding
ears. Small eye. Narrow, long head.

Desirable and
undesirable shapes,
1977.

Peter Gurney feeding a pair of guinea pigs.

Thanks, in some measure, to Gurney's promotion of them, guinea pigs are now among the most popular small companion animals, and the fundamentals of their care are widely understood and disseminated – for example, that at least two should be kept together for company; that they should not be housed with rabbits, whose diets are different and which may injure their hutchmates by kicking them; and that they need to receive a sure supply of vitamin C, either in their food or through supplements. A quick search on the web will throw up a host of pictures, anecdotes and names – although few of the latter can match the heroic roster compiled by u.s. President Theodore Roosevelt's children for their pets: Bishop Doane, Dr Johnson, Father G. Grady, Fighting Bob Evans and Admiral Dewey.[11]

Today's guinea pigs are exposed to all the lures of consumerism – or, rather, their owners are. My own animals ate a mixture of oats and bran, supplemented with their bedding hay, grass (when they ran on the lawn), dandelion leaves and the outer leaves of cabbages that I was allowed to pick up free from our local greengrocer's. Now they would be offered such delights as Burgess Excel Complete Food Cubes, 'A blend of Timothy hay, tasty blackcurrant flavours and oregano oil, combined with the perfect balance of vitamins, minerals and high fibre nuggets', which 'will give your guinea pig everything it needs for dental, digestive and emotional health, in a single conveniently portioned cube'. The popular UK petshop chain Pets at Home lists 22 'Boredom Breaker' products for guinea pigs on its website (although, to be fair, many of these are also suitable for other small pets such as rabbits and hamsters). A modern guinea pig can stave off boredom by nibbling on a Woodlands Coconut and Rope Chew, try its hand at gardening in a Veg Play Patch ('made from sisal, straw and corn leaf and coloured with pet safe vegetable dyes'), wriggle through an Adventure Tunnel, puzzle out how to extract its food from a Small Animal Kong toy, and finally retire to bed with an Organic Bed

A cigarette card shows how (or rather, how *not*) to hold a guinea pig.

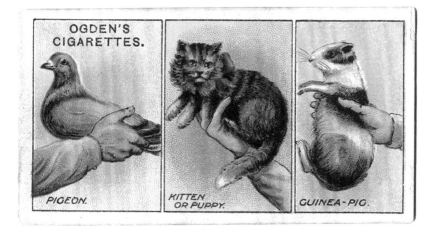

Buddie (a fabric carrot). All these products are fun, and harmless, but collectively rather heavy on the purse.

As mentioned above, pet guides recommend frequent handling of guinea pigs, provided this is done sensitively and the animal's preferences are respected. With regular handling goes close observation and an appreciation of distinctive behaviours. The guinea pig fraternity is bound closer by the special words invented to describe some of these. *Popcorning*, for example, is usually seen in baby guinea pigs, but also in adults: the animal runs around excitedly and leaps in the air, lands on all four feet, then quickly turns in another direction and repeats the jump. *Barbering* is the trimming of the hair of a companion animal. Peter Gurney, who noticed this in his pets, was impressed by

> the neatness of the trimming and how nicely balanced the hair length [was] either side . . . I had one amazing example of one of a litter of three, a sow, barbering her sister, brother

A pet shop guinea pig waits for a buyer.

Guinea pigs as consumers.

and her mother. I first noticed it when the 'barber' was about ten days old, and by the time she had been weaned, about four weeks later, the rest of her family were very well shorn![12]

(Such behaviour is the bane of owners of show-standard Peruvians, who may spend months grooming their pets only to discover them one morning with a 'short back and sides'.) 'Rumblestrutting' (also called 'motorboating') is exactly that – pacing around another guinea pig, swaying the hips from side to side and making a throaty, rumbling sound. Both males and females rumblestrut, and although it is a way of bidding for dominance it does not necessarily precede overtly aggressive behaviour.

Guinea pigs have a whole repertoire of cries and calls – in fact, decoding and responding to their 'language' is agreed to be one of the greatest pleasures in looking after them. One of the oddest, rarest and least explained is the bird-like 'song'. As Peter Gurney describes it,

At first, there is a short, sharp panting of breath – 'ha, ha, ha, ha!' – and then gradually the vocal chords are brought into play. At this stage, all the other guinea pigs in the vicinity will freeze. From then on, there is an ethereal quality about the performance. The guinea pig making the noise usually raises its head high and gives the appearance of being in a trance-like state. Its companions will either look towards it or stand transfixed, staring ahead. It can last for a minute or carry on for a few minutes.[13]

One theory is that the 'singing' is stress related, but Gurney noted that it always occurred during quiet periods, when there was no apparent threat to the group.

As well as the community of pet owners, there is also a thriving network of clubs and societies, which arrange an annual calendar of guinea pig shows (although, as previously mentioned, they tend to prefer the term 'cavy'). The exhibiting of guinea pigs has been going on for more than a century, but in the late 1970s the British Cavy Council was set up to establish standards for each of the recognized breeds. There are two kinds of standard: Full Standards are 'for all breeds of cavy that in the council's opinion represent varieties that are *distinct from all other existing breeds*, provide *a desirable addition to the Cavy Fancy*, and for which a *standard of excellence has been established and agreed* after a sustained process of breeding and exhibition'. Guide Standards are more provisional and are for 'breeds of cavy that are in a *process of development*'.[14] Full Standard breeds are divided into the following (with explanatory notes and examples): Self (shorthaired, solid-coloured), Ticked (shorthaired with each individual hair containing two distinct shades, such as the Agouti or Argente), Marked (shorthaired with specifically placed markings, for example Dutch, Tortoiseshell, Harlequin, Magpie or Belted),

Marked Pattern (shorthaired with markings in a defined pattern,
for example Himalayan, Fox), Crested (any variant with a crest on
its head), Satin (any variant with a satinized coat), Rough-coated
Shorthair (for example Abyssinian, Rex, Teddy), Longhair (for
example Sheltie or, in the u.s., Silkie, Peruvian, Merino, Alpaca).
Within each of these groups there are approved colours – lilac,
silver, buff, cinnamon, chocolate and so on – creating a finely
differentiated rainbow of shades, patterns and textures.

In competition marks are awarded out of 100, but for each
breed the weighting is different, so that, for example, the 'feel' of
the coat of the Rex, ideally dense, springy and resilient, is worth
45 points, nearly half the total. A Tortoiseshell, by contrast, can
garner up to 60 points for its markings, which are to consist of

'patches of black and red, evenly distributed on each side of the body on either side of a central "line" formed by the meeting of patches of different colours'. The basic requirement is, of course, a healthy animal with a good temperament (*animals that prove difficult to handle or control, or that show clear signs of aggression, should be penalised, with Disqualification being appropriate in extreme cases*'). Some of the specified faults, such as running lice, missing eyes, a wry neck or laboured breathing, appear so gross that it seems a wonder that anyone would try to exhibit a guinea pig suffering from them. Others, however, are more esoteric: side whiskers or rosettes in the coat would result in the instant ousting of a smooth shorthair. And the council adds a memo in emboldened type that 'Both Hairless and so-called "Skinny" cavies may not be shown at any cavy show held in the United Kingdom.' Judges are instructed to eject them immediately. (The situation is different in Scandinavia, where hairless breeds *are* sometimes admitted to the show table. The allocation of points that must take place rather boggles the imagination.)

The cavy 'fancy' (which the *Oxford English Dictionary* defines as 'The art or practice of breeding animals so as to develop points of conventional beauty or excellence') is a self-regulated world and decides for itself what is meritorious and what is not – a circular process, as the requirement for new breeds to do no more than provide 'a desirable addition to the Cavy Fancy' implies. There is no pre-existing 'perfect' model of a guinea pig that the exhibitors aspire to, for, as we have seen, guinea pigs are whatever we wish to make them. Still, as one reads through the British Cavy Council's 70-page 'Breed Standards' document, some themes emerge. First, the bodies of the guinea pigs are subjected to a global scrutiny in which even the smallest physical detail can mean the difference between success and failure. Satin guinea pigs should not have white toenails (unless their coat colour is white) or areas of darker pigmentation on the rims of their ears. The black, red and white patches on Tortoise & Whites must be 'clearly defined from surrounding patches, and with no intermingling of hairs of a different colour'. However, since a fault seen on the 'top side of the cavy has a greater adverse impact on the overall appearance than one which is "hidden" underneath,

Judgement day.

Glenwhilks Daydream, a long-haired Sheltie, double champion, owned by Ann Johnston of Glenwhilk Cavies.

preference should be given to a cavy with a good top and less good under than one with the opposite characteristics'. (This precisely locates the human in relation to the animal: above, looking down. A similar perspective is taken on the English Self, which, viewed from on high, should give the 'impression . . . of a brick, rounded at the corners'.)

A show-winning Abyssinian will display:

Four rosettes in direct line across the body, these being the saddle and side rosettes.
A rosette on each hip in line with each other.
Two thumb-shaped rump rosettes with equal centres.

The 'thumb-shaped rump rosettes' bring in another key element – 'handling'. As well as being looked at, show guinea pigs are stroked to assess the quality of their coat, which, as we have seen, is a crucially important marker for several breeds. Hairs are parted to check that their colour goes all the way down to the skin. And the desirable quality of 'cobbyness', which is very often mentioned, suggests a plump, stocky body that fits satisfyingly between the palms. Visual and tactile rewards come together in the assessment of the Satin, whose hollow hair shafts give it 'the gloss-painted coat of the guinea pig world'.[15] 'To assess the degree and quality of the sheen', the judge is instructed to 'handle the cavy in such a way that the coat "catches the light" to its fullest advantage'.

Breeding and exhibiting guinea pigs gives pleasure to many people, and the cherished and radiantly healthy animals that ascend to the winners' podium are undoubtedly a charming sight. How might the guinea pigs themselves rate the show experience? It is probable that they enjoy the extra grooming and personal attention from their owners – at least, if they did not, they would

Glenwhilks Tricie, a Dutch cavy, twice Best of Breed, owned by Debbie and Agnes of Glenwhilk Cavies.

voice their annoyance and would not be taken to a show at all. Minor inconveniences, from their point of view, might include the withdrawal of some of their favourite foods (carrots, for example, stain the mouth area); the removal, by brushing, of the guard hairs on their coats, which are thought to be unsightly; or, if they are Peruvians, being dressed in origami-like paper 'wrappers' so that their unfeasibly long hair (which can grow to more than 18 inches (45 cm) long) is kept clear of the ground. The show environment is arranged to cause them the least possible stress – food, water and hay are provided, and stewards keep an eye on their welfare.

A more substantial objection is the one that is also expressed with regard to pedigree dogs – that controlled reproduction results in genetic changes that are actually harmful. Roan guinea pigs, for instance, must not be allowed to mate with each other, for a high proportion of their offspring will be born with tiny eyes (microphthalmic) and teeth problems, and will soon die. The same is true of spotted Dalmations (spelled that way, unlike the dog breed). There is also some concern over the breeding of Satins, which seem to be prone to osteodystrophy, a degenerative bone disease.

What does the future hold for the 'fancy'? The wilder shores of cavydom do not only host the nearly bald 'Skinnies': there are also the corkscrew-curled Lunkaryas (pronounced *lunka-ree-as*), who descend from a longhaired curly male called Prince Adam, owned by Monica and Annica Lundqvist, who ran a pet shop in Stockholm in the 1980s. Their name is a blend of 'Lundqvist' and *rya*, the Swedish word for 'sheep'. And then there is the Sheba, or Sheba Mini Yak (also known as the 'Bad Hair Day' cavy), which was bred by Wynne Eecen in the 1970s and is now a recognized breed in its native Australia.[16] And doubtless many more – although which, if any, will officially be elevated to the dignity of Full Breed Status is anybody's guess.

7 Heroes and Heroines

Although guinea pigs are less common characters than squirrels, rabbits, or mice, they still feature in such a large number of children's books and films that what follows can only be a selection.

In Lewis Carroll's *Alice's Adventures in Wonderland*, two guinea pigs are among the crowd of outraged animals who gather round the unfortunate lizard Bill after he has been kicked up and out of a chimney by the oversized Alice. They revive him with brandy, and later reappear among the jurors assembled at the trial of the Knave of Hearts ('Who stole the tarts?') – although not for long:

> Here one of the guinea-pigs cheered, and was immediately suppressed by the officers of the court. (As that is rather a hard word, I will just explain to you how it was done. They had a large canvas bag, which tied up at the mouth with strings: into this they slipped the guinea-pig, head first, and then sat upon it.)

The other guinea pig is dealt with in the same way, but receives no sympathy from Alice, who is simply pleased that she now knows what 'suppressing' someone means. "'Come, that finished the guinea-pigs!" thought Alice. "Now we shall get on better."' It was probably Carroll's love of wordplay that conjured up these

victims of process, for in his day members of a jury might be jokingly referred to as 'guinea pigs'.

An even worse fate than being 'suppressed' awaits the seven young guinea pigs in Edward Lear's nonsense story 'The History of the Seven Families of the Lake Pipple-Popple' (the lake is on the outskirts of the city of Tosh). Although their parents had advised them to eat lettuces 'not greedily but calmly', they are so enthused by the appearance of 'a large Lettuce which had grown out of the ground where they had been sleeping' in a garden 'full of Gooseberry Bushes and Tiggory Trees' that they rush at it with extreme force. Collision with the lettuce stalk brings on concussion and an 'incipient transitional inflammation of their noses which grew worse and worse and worse and worse till it incidentally killed them all Seven'. Their parents, who discover their fate 'through reading in the newspapers', immediately arrange for their own pickling, and are displayed in the museum of Tosh 'for the daily inspection and contemplation and for the perpetual benefit of the pusillanimous public'.

Lear's drawing of the deceased young guinea pigs is echoed by – and no doubt influenced – the opening illustration of Beatrix

126

Beatrix Potter, 'There once was an amiable guinea pig', from *Appley Dapply's Nursery Rhymes* (1917).

Beatrix Potter, 'He wore a sweet tie', from *Appley Dapply's Nursery Rhymes*.

Potter's *The Tale of the Flopsy Bunnies*, which shows the bunnies slumped in a circle after the 'soporific' effects of eating too much lettuce. Both stories tell of the dire consequences of greed for small animals (the slumbering bunnies are popped into a sack by Mr McGregor), but Potter makes sure her little characters are rescued before being skinned or sold for 'baccy'.

Although the Flopsy Bunnies survive, we have seen from the case of the unfortunate Queen Elizabeth that Potter's attitude to her animal subjects was briskly unsentimental. However, she clearly valued the sketches she had made of Nina Paget's crew, for one of them, with ruffled white hair, which he brushes into place 'like a periwig', appears more than twenty years later in *Appley Dapply's Nursery Rhymes* (1917), carefully titivating himself in front of a mirror before stepping out in sky-blue tie, top hat and spats. In *Cecily Parsley's Nursery Rhymes* (1922) four guinea pigs with brown and white 'Dutch' markings tend a vegetable bed (in which lettuces, of course, are planted), busily raking and digging under the watchful eye of an older animal in a long coat and pince-nez.

In 1903, while she and her brother Bertram were on holiday in Hastings during 'a *very* wet week', Potter had sketched out a story

Beatrix Potter,
'And his whiskers
and buttons were
very big', from
*Appley Dapply's
Nursery Rhymes.*

about a guinea pig called Tuppenny. It is set in 'the land of Green
Ginger', in 'a town called Marmalade, which is exclusively inhabited by guinea pigs'. They 'are of all colours, and of two sorts – the
common ordinary smooth-haired guinea-pigs who run errands
and keep greengrocers shops – and the kind that call themselves
Abyssinian Cavies – who wear ringlets and walk upon their toes'.
The former 'admire and envy the curls of the long-haired guinea-
pigs', which are combed and trimmed by the town's barber, 'but
he cannot do very much for the smooth-haired guinea-pigs –
except apply pomatum – which has no effect, only making their
smooth hair even flatter than it was before'. The cunning barber
makes up a new hair-wash called Quintessence of Abyssinian
Artichokes, which he claims is so powerful it would 'cause aspara -
gus to grow upon a doorknob' (and will also cure chicken pox).
The Abyssinian Cavies are disgusted at this threat to their social
superiority, and spread a rumour that the potion is 'made of

slugs'. However, this does not discourage the short-hairs from paying for a miserable individual called Tuppenny to be treated (the barber squirts him with a garden syringe 'in order not to wet his own hands'). After a long wait, Tuppenny's hair *does* grow, but in a 'perfectly frightful' way. The barber cannot keep up with trimming it, so 'his family cut it themselves with scissors, all crooked and jagged behind, and stuffed pincushions with the snippings'. Eventually, poor Tuppenny, plagued by 'rude little guinea-pig boys' who run after him shouting 'old whiskers!!', sells himself to 'a travelling showman; who goes about the country with a tent; and a brass band; and a menagerie of five Polecats and Weasels; and a troupe of performing fleas; and the Fat Dormouse of Salisbury; and TUPPENNY the HAIRY GUINEA-pig who lives in a caravan!'[1]

In 1929 Tuppenny reappeared as the hero of *The Fairy Caravan*, a loosely connected series of anecdotes celebrating the characters, scenes and traditions of Potter's beloved Lake District. The book grew out of her friendship with Henry P. Coolidge, a thirteen-year-old American boy who visited her at Hill Top with his mother, Gail,

Beatrix Potter, 'We have a little garden', from *Cecily Parsley's Nursery Rhymes* (1922).

in 1927. It is dedicated to him, and he appears in the opening chapter as one of Tuppenny's friends. Potter's own guinea pig (another 'Tuppenny') had just died, and when Gail Coolidge returned to London she bought two long-haired guinea pigs from Harrods and arranged for them to be sent to Hill Top. They were welcomed warmly and, although they were both female, were christened Henry P. and Mrs Tuppenny.

The Fairy Caravan (1929) was published by an American publisher, although Potter arranged for 100 unbound sets to be made up by an Ambleside printer in order to establish her copyright in the UK. The first British edition did not appear until 1952. Although it has not been treated kindly by critics, the story has a gentle, rambling attractiveness, shot through here and there with a tart wit, as in the portrait of the insufferably 'purry' tabby cat Mary Ellen. It is imbued with Potter's deep affinity

Beatrix Potter, 'And tend it with such care', from *Cecily Parsley's Nursery Rhymes*.

Abyssinian aristocrats, and commoners, from Beatrix Potter, *The Fairy Caravan* (1929).

with individual animals – not only the Tuppennies, but Sandy, the circus proprietor, who is the West Highland terrier she kept as a child, and Xarifa the dormouse, another childhood companion (and one who had the distinction of being petted by John Everett Millais).

The first chapter of *The Fairy Caravan* follows *The Tale of Tuppenny* quite closely, although there are some changes. The deceitful barber has been replaced by two shysters called Ratton and Scratch, who set up a booth selling bottles of a wonderful 'hair elixir'. Henry P. and several others buy a bottle, which they pour over their friend Tuppenny, reasoning that his appearance can hardly be made worse – he suffers from chilblains and his hair is thin and patchy, possibly from ill-treatment. The uncontrollable growth that results is vigorously attacked by Mrs Tuppenny, who 'cut it, and cut it, and stuffed pin-cushions with it, and pillow cases and bolsters'. Eventually she lays her scissors aside and starts to tweak it out instead, which is the last straw for her husband who, like his earlier namesake, flees from Marmalade to join the circus. However, this is not the rackety band of polecats, weasels and fleas, but the company of the Fairy Caravan, who travel round the countryside staging performances for animals. Tuppenny's flowing locks (which have

Ratton and Scratch sell hair elixir, from Beatrix Potter, *The Fairy Caravan.*

now stopped growing) are a positive asset in his new role as the Sultan of Zanzibar. Although the focus of the book now shifts from him, and he is present merely as the audience for tales told by the other animals ('you must understand there is not so much exclusively guinea pig in the other later chapters', Potter wrote to Henry P.), it is clear that Tuppenny has found his vocation, along with health and happiness (those chilblains have disappeared). His previous wretched condition perhaps harks back to Nina Paget's 'infinite' hordes (also the source, of course, of his new name) –

among the tribe at 28 Bolton Gardens, there were very likely a poorly and downtrodden few.

There are a few hints in the story that guinea pigs themselves were not wholly familiar to everyone. It is 'the rarity of guinea-pigs', as well as his remarkable hair, that makes Tuppenny such a welcome addition to the circus, while Sandy has to explain his nature to the owner of the milliner's shop where he is buying Tuppenny a costume befitting his new role (he was 'worthy of considerable outlay by way of dressing up'): 'A guinea pig! is that a species of wild boar, Mr Sandy? Does it bite?' 'No, no! A most genteel and timid animal, Miss Louisa.'

In C. S. Lewis's *The Magician's Nephew* (1955), the sixth book published in his Narnia series but actually a prequel to the events narrated in *The Lion, the Witch and the Wardrobe*, would-be sorcerer Andrew Ketterley attempts to reach another universe by experimenting on guinea pigs:

'Some of them only died. Some exploded like little bombs –'.

'It was a jolly cruel thing to do,' said Digory who had once had a guinea-pig of his own.

'How you do keep getting off the point!' said Uncle Andrew. 'That's what the creatures were for. I'd bought them myself.'

Tuppenny's troublesome hair, from Beatrix Potter, *The Fairy Caravan.*

Uncle Andrew's heartless treatment of the guinea pigs evokes the long-running debate on the morality of experimenting on live animals. In a story in which the godlike lion Aslan populates the new world of Narnia with characterful and rational Talking Beasts, his crime appears particularly unforgivable. When Digory and Polly arrive in the Wood between the Worlds they find one of the experimental guinea pigs, 'nosing about in the grass'. At Polly's suggestion – 'It's perfectly happy here, and your uncle will only do something horrid to it if we take it home' – they leave it where it is. The Wood, with its leafy green daylight and unbroken quiet, is a portal through which other universes can be reached – 'not really a place at all', according to some. The guinea pigs (hopefully plural) therefore become pleasingly anomalous elements within Lewis's cosmology.

Jean-Pierre, the hero of a series of books by Paul Gallico – *The Day the Guinea-Pig Talked* (1963), *The Day Jean-Pierre was Pignapped* (1964), *The Day Jean-Pierre Went Round the World* (1965), *The Day Jean-Pierre Joined the Circus* (1969) – is an Abyssinian guinea pig, 'something like a cross between a clothes brush and a feather duster'. He lives with his owner, Cecile, on her parents' flower farm near Cannes in the south of France, although he also has a spell as a star turn in a circus, performing with the motherly kangaroo Angelique. In the first story he and Cecile are able to talk to each other in the magic space of time 'between twelve o'clock' while the clock is striking. They both choose to say 'I love you', and their devotion to each other is a key theme. Their secret place is an old cellar, and in particular the stone shelf on which Cecile places Jean-Pierre in order to commune with him:

> when Cecile had to look down upon Jean-Pierre all she could see was his browny back with its black marking somewhat in the shape of a potato.

And when Jean-Pierre had to look up at Cecile, all *he* could see were her legs going up past her knees and into her skirts like two thin tree-trunks.

But when Cecile put Jean-Pierre on the stone shelf in the cellar it was just right. In this way they could look at one another face to face for as long as they liked.[2]

Michael Bond's much-loved adventures of Olga da Polga started off as 'not much more than a record of a typical day in the life of a guinea-pig, describing how she lived, what she ate, how to build a hutch and an outdoor run'.[3] The original Olga was bought for Bond's daughter Karen, and was named simply because 'the children who lived next door had one they called

A joyous
Olga da Polga,
by Hans Helweg.

Boris'. However, although the stories follow the day-to-day life of an average pet – taken to a show, having her toenails clipped, accidentally falling out of her hutch – what gives them lift-off is the contrast between these plain facts and Olga's bravura imagination. Addicted to the telling of Munchausen-like tall tales – and described by the *Times Literary Supplement* as having 'a touch of Bunter and Falstaff' about her – she squeezes under the frame of her run to explore the 'Elysian fields' that Fangio, the hedgehog from a nearby garage ('they do say he has Argentine blood'), has told her about. Shut in a shed on 5 November, she relates how, in the dim and distant past (BD, Before Dandelions), guinea pigs reached the moon by climbing on to each other's shoulders to form a huge but wobbly tower (their characteristic 'Wheeeeeee' squeak being a handed-down memory of that tower's collapse).

The original Boris appears too, 'transferred for purposes of plot from his hutch in the house next door to a more impressive abode near the sea, where he lived in some splendour'. In the final chapter of *Olga Meets Her Match*, Olga's sojourn with him results in the arrival of three babies, to her own complete surprise. Boris's role in this is tactfully handled: the most we see him do is 'snuggle closer' to Olga and murmur 'My princess' as they lie side by side in the grass. However, even this was too much for a potential American co-publisher, who wrote to Bond saying that 'if they were to take the book they would like me to insert a few paragraphs allowing Olga the opportunity to discuss with Boris the possibility of having a family before the two of them retired for the night.'[4] Bond retorted that this would be totally out of character for Boris, who is a male chauvinist pig in every sense; another publisher was found, and Olga flourished not only in the United States but in many other countries around the world (including France, where she is known as Charlotte Parlotte).

Hans Helweg's line drawings brilliantly celebrate Olga's boundless *joie de vivre*. Some of the stories have recently been reissued by Oxford University Press, with new illustrations by Catherine Rayner. Rayner's Olga was partly based on photographs of her own guinea pig, Marvin, and partly on Michael Bond's own Olga (the fourth of that name), 'a beautiful tri-coloured Abyssinian'. She wanted to make her 'quirky and fun', while still keeping 'the opinion she has of herself as "a little guinea to be taken seriously"'. She is also distracted by her imagination and in a little bubble of her own.'[5] Rayner's lively decoration of the margins with sprays of wild flowers, toadstools and tiny insects encourages us to look at the world from Olga's point of view. She advances, nose forward, intent on exploring its delights, the daisy pattern on her coat showing she is truly part of it.

Charlotte Middleton's guinea pig Christopher is a miniature eco-warrior who remedies a shortage of dandelions (eaten to near-extinction by his friends and relations) by carefully nurturing the last surviving plant, which he finds under his bedroom window. His adventures, in *Christopher Nibble* (2009), *Christopher's Caterpillars* (2012) and *Christopher's Bicycle* (2013), all published by Oxford University Press, are designed to encourage 'young children to think about what they eat, conservation, and ecological awareness – all important life skills to develop from the earliest age'. Many of the charming illustrations are in a collage style, from the bug-surrounded cabbages that the guinea pigs scorn to Christopher's 'enviable wardrobe of patterned shorts', and readers are invited to make their own pictures using 'fabrics, patterned papers, and even pressed flowers'. Also, like Christopher, they are reminded of the simple pleasure of blowing the seedlings from dandelion clocks – although hopefully not over their parents' flowerbeds.

Guinea pigs also appear in a number of children's TV programmes and films. Fans of early science fiction may have noticed that Hamlet, the space-travelling hamster in the TV series *Pathfinders*, is actually played by a white guinea pig. In the fourth episode of *Pathfinders to Mars* ('Lichens', broadcast 1 January 1961), Hamlet has to wait to become the first small rodent to set foot on the Red Planet while a suitably sized spacesuit is made for him. However, the limits of his talent are exposed in a scene in which he is supposed to register alarm at an approaching sandstorm. 'Look at Hamlet! He's frightened! He's sensed something!' one of the characters exclaims – but the accompanying shot shows the actor simply ambling to and fro.

For British viewers of a certain age, the seductively pattering guitar melody from the Andante in C Major by Mauro Giuliani instantly brings to mind *Tales of the Riverbank*, a long-running series in which a clutch of small animals – Hammy Hamster, Roderick the Water Rat and G.P. the Guinea Pig – embark on a series of adventures, often involving miniature cars, boats, aeroplanes and even a diving bell.

Tales of the Riverbank was created for Canadian television by David Ellison and Paul Sutherland, but when CBC turned down the production after a pilot episode it was commissioned by the BBC. The initial series (thirteen episodes in black and white) first aired in Britain on 3 July 1960. Since the BBC preferred the animals not to speak with Canadian accents, the voices – all of them – were provided by the children's presenter Johnny Morris. Morris characterized the boastful G.P. with no-nonsense Northern tones that, to some ears, resemble those of the Yorkshire and England cricketer and radio commentator Geoffrey Boycott.

The series proved immensely popular: it was eventually sold to 34 countries around the world and was succeeded by 39 more episodes in black and white and a further 26 in colour (by which time, in the 1970s, the title had been changed to *Hammy Hamster*); this last series was re-screened in the 1990s by Channel 4 as *Further*

Tales of the Riverbank. In the United States, a late-night showing called *Once Upon a Hamster* attracted a cult following, watched, according to Paul Sutherland's obituary in the *Toronto Star* (20 May 2004), by musicians returning home from their gigs. The U.S. television producer Alan Ball paid his own tribute by including a clip showing G.P. appearing on a TV screen in one episode of the hit HBO series *Six Feet Under*. And a film, *Tales of the Riverbank*, was made in 2008, with the voices of Steve Coogan as Roderick, Ardal O'Hanlon as Hammy and Jim Broadbent as G.P. ('a retired Major, one of nature's organisers, but perhaps a little less organised than a real Major would be', is how Broadbent describes him on the film's website).

David Ellison, long-term writer and director of the various TV series, has spoken about the various ploys which were used to persuade the animals to 'perform' (they were first filmed at high speed with a slower playback, which made their movements appear more deliberate). The chosen actors, which naturally had to be replaced as the runs extended, were all female, partly so that they would be more placid and therefore easier to handle, and partly, in G.P.'s case, because a smaller guinea pig would minimize the size difference with the hamster (or hamsters – a number were used per episode in the hope of getting an hour or two of daylight work out of each before it fell asleep). Jam was smeared on objects which the animals were required to handle, or to nibble, and facial expressiveness was achieved by discreetly blowing on their noses. Ellison describes G.P., in his highly desirable watermill home, as a sort of 'mad professor', and credits the series' enduring appeal to its portrayal of 'the kindness and gentleness of a community'.[6]

'The Trouble with Tribbles' (first broadcast 29 December 1967) reprises Ellis Parker Butler's story 'Pigs is Pigs' as a challenge for the crew of the Starship *Enterprise*. David Gerrold, the writer of the *Star Trek* episode, originally argued that he had simply recrafted the 'rabbits in Australia' story as an ecological fable, replacing the rabbits with easy-to-model fluff balls, but he later admitted that he had been influenced by Robert Heinlein's 1952 science fiction novel, *The Rolling Stones*. In Heinlein's tale, the Stone twins, Castor and Pollux, are persuaded to buy a 'flat cat' by a shopkeeper on Mars: the 'cat', a 'pie-shaped mass of sleek red fur', purrs companionably when it is tickled. On board the family space ship it gives birth to eight kittens, each of which quickly reproduces again (flat cats are born already pregnant). The Stones solve the problem by putting all the animals in cold storage, where they hibernate; they are subsequently revived and sold as pets to lonely miners in the asteroid belt. Heinlein acknowledged his own debt to 'Pigs is Pigs', and generously waived any recompense from the *Star Trek* team, asking only for an autographed copy of the script.[7]

The *Star Trek* tribbles are bundles of fluff, with no externally visible features. Humans are irresistibly drawn to them and they seem to have 'a tranquillizing effect on the human nervous system'. In 'The Trouble with Tribbles', Lieutenant Uhura receives one from a travelling pedlar called Cyrano Jones and brings it aboard the *Enterprise*. Here it gives birth, and soon there are tribbles everywhere (1,771,561 of them, according to Mr Spock's impeccable calculations). Leonard McCoy discovers that tribbles are bisexual and, like the flat cats, are already pregnant when they are born – in fact, 50 per cent of their metabolism is given over to reproduction. Although they usually emit a cosy purr, they shriek with alarm when they encounter a Klingon; Klingons in turn consider them to be 'mortal enemies' of the Klingon empire. Spock, too, fails to find them endearing, arguing that they fulfil no logical purpose ('They toil not, neither do they spin . . .'). Their one good point is that they 'do not talk too much'. Despite the chaos they cause, the tribbles eventually save the day: the fact that many of them die after devouring the contents of a grain store shows that the grain had been poisoned, and their shrieking and shaking unmasks a disguised Klingon agent. They end up being beamed over to the engine room of the Klingon ship, where Scotty happily declares 'they'll be no tribble at all'.

The tribbles can be seen as guinea pigs reduced to the most basic of caricatures: a rounded shape with flowing hair like the Peruvian breed, an insatiable appetite (when they are not reproducing they are eating) and a phenomenal ability to increase in number (hence the expression 'multiplying like tribbles' in sci-fi contexts). Many people's favourite scene in 'The Trouble with Tribbles' is the one in which a bemused Kirk emerges from an avalanche of them after he has unwittingly opened a storage hatch above which they have been massing. *Star Trek* lore has it that after the first deluge, certain cast members aimed extra tribbles at William Shatner's head in the hope that he would break out of character.

Captain Kirk overcome by tribbles.

In 'Pandemic 2: The Startling' (2008), an episode from season 12 of the U.S. cartoon series *South Park*, giant guinea pigs rampage around New York to the accompaniment of parodically shaky camera work and keynote cries of 'I'm so . . . *startled!*' It turns out that they can only be kept at bay by the roving panpipe bands that the government has rounded up and dispatched to Guantánamo Bay. At the story's climax, the evil Director of Homeland Security is unmasked as a guinea-pirate – we've previously been treated to guinea-bees, guinea-rabbits and a guinea-saurus-rex, all of them real animals encased in colourful felt costumes. Creators Trey Parker and Matt Stone found it hard to persuade the guinea pigs to move – their instinct, once dressed up and therefore in an unfamiliar situation, was to sit still – but they had no difficulty finding the costumes themselves, which were handmade in a town in Pennsylvania by Terry Smoker of Cuddly Cavies Creations (and can still be bought, complete with 'diapers', which 'will allow you to enjoy spending time with a guinea pig that might have urination issues'). Guinea pig fashions are also crafted by Maki Yamada, who offers traditional Japanese as well as Halloween and Santa Claus outfits.[8]

The Disney film *G-Force* (2009), featuring special agents Darwin, Juarez and Blaster, was a smash hit, reaching No. 1 in the box office and taking around $300 million worldwide. Although the computer-animated stars scuttle off on all fours when they are required to move at speed, they often rise up on their hind legs, their widely planted feet giving them a passing resemblance to Wild West gunslingers, especially since they are often decked out with an assortment of weaponry.

Guinea pigs have also featured in advertising campaigns, perhaps the best known being the U.S. 'Carl and Ray' series, in which a pet shop rabbit and guinea pig marvel at the tremendous deals on offer in the Blockbuster Video outlet opposite their

Poster for the film *G-Force* (2009).

142

window. The short films were aired in 2002–3, with a later episode, in which the two try to get online by repeatedly prodding an actual mouse, being voted the best advert to be shown during Superbowl 2007 ('We didn't plug it in', Ray concludes, dangling his victim by the tail – to which the mouse instantly retorts, 'Don't even think about it!'). However, the ads also attracted some criticism for suggesting to literal-minded viewers that rabbits and guinea pigs could be kept together.

Modern guinea pig heroes and heroines are unlikely to parade the overt moral messages that their nineteenth-century counterparts did, although we do see them being used to instil respect for the living, growing world, as in the 'Christopher Nibble' books. Their appeal as fictional characters is heightened by their familiarity as pets, whether owned by children themselves or met in the school classroom, a pet shop, a farm park or at the zoo. There

'Kimono' costume by Maki Yamada.

'Ninja' costume by Maki Yamada.

145

is really no limit to the roles that guinea pigs can play, and comedy often springs from the contrast between their placid demeanour and the outlandish adventures they become involved in. There is only one gap that I can think of: *South Park* aside, I have yet to meet an anti-hero – a truly *evil* guinea pig.

8 Tailpiece

Once, according to Olga da Polga, guinea pigs had 'the most marvellous tails imaginable. Long and thick, with fur like silky-cream.' One day, clustered at the border between Peru and its one-time neighbour, the fairy-tale kingdom of Barsance, they see a prince trying to climb up a sheer rock, at the top of which a beautiful princess has been imprisoned in a tower by her evil stepfather. Generously, the guinea pigs sacrifice their tails to make a silken rope, which the prince uses to scale the rockface after a helpful eagle has carried it to the princess so she can tie it to the bars of her prison.[1]

Olga's tall tale could be read as a parable, for guinea pigs' contact with the human world has resulted in changes to their bodies, to their habitat and to their behaviour, too. *Cavia porcellus* is a species created to serve human needs and is kept in existence because it continues to be of use to us. It is an apt representative of this latest era in the Earth's history, the Anthropocene, in which, in Caspar Henderson's words, 'as we increasingly reshape Creation through science and technology, not to mention our sheer numbers, the creatures that do thrive and evolve are, increasingly, corollaries of our values and concerns.'[2]

Yet we have not quite succeeded in pinning guinea pigs down. I began this book with another story about them, in which humans tied themselves in knots because they couldn't agree on what to call them. That indeterminacy, a way of squeezing through the barriers and eluding definition, is also a part of their history. A lot of what we think we know about them has to be qualified in one way or another. For example, although we think of them as rodents, in the 1990s some scientists argued that this classification is wrong, and that 'the Caviomorpha [a group that includes chinchillas and degus as well as guinea pigs] should be elevated in taxonomical rank and regarded as a separate mammalian order distinct from the Rodentia.'[3] Even if they *are* rodents (and the consensus now is that they are) they are most unusual ones, with their atypically lengthy pregnancies, their inability to make their own vitamin C and their production of a form of insulin which differs from that of other mammals in its growth-promoting functions.

Again, the general opinion of guinea pigs, passed down over the centuries, is that they are amiable but dim. They are 'so stupid', Thomas Bewick declared, 'as to allow themselves to be killed by cats, without resistance. They pass their whole lives in sleeping,

The author's first guinea pig.

ADD HOT WATER AND SERVE

"ROTOGRAPH" SERIES

Copyright 1905 by the Rotograph Co. N.Y.

B 1711

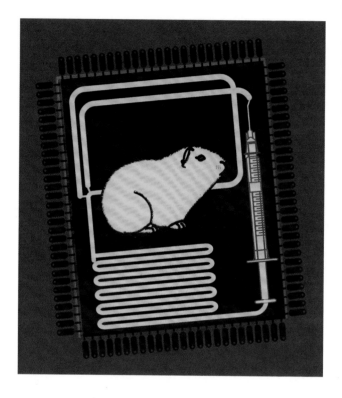

The Silicon Guinea Pig, heralding computer chips that mimic living organisms.

eating, and in the propagation of their species. They are by nature gentle and tame: They do no mischief but seem to be equally incapable of good.'[4] Theodore Roosevelt agreed. Although he himself had a soft spot for his children's pets, and wrote in a letter that he was presently 'acting as nurse to two wee guinea pigs' belonging to his daughter, he had no scruples about declaring that the intellect of his successor in the White House, William Howard Taft, fell slightly shy of a guinea pig's, or that the 'hopeless' British ambassador, Sir Henry Mortimer Durand, 'seems to have a brain of about eight-guinea-pig-power'.[5]

This prejudice was shared by scientists, who mistook the characteristically wary behaviour of a prey species for stupidity:

> A guinea pig will gnaw for five minutes at a freely swinging door without happening to give it a hard enough push to open it. The gentle swinging of the door back and forth seemed to suggest nothing . . . Even though extremely hungry the little fellow will get discouraged after finding that all the methods he knows fail to reach the food, and he will sit down in a corner of the cage and remain there.[6]

Consequently, although guinea pigs have proved able to navigate simple labyrinths, and to discriminate between different stimuli, researchers investigating learning and memory in rodents have generally ignored them, preferring to use rats and mice instead.

Behind the low estimate of guinea pig intelligence lies the assumption that domesticated animals are less bright and

A guinea pig badge created for a competition at the British Museum.

resourceful than wild ones because their simplified environment means they do not need to think very hard. It is true that a reduction in brain size is one of the physiological changes seen in guinea pigs – their brains are about 13 per cent smaller than comparable wild cavies. However, it does not follow that they possess a lesser amount of intelligence – which is, after all, a many-stranded concept. In a recent experiment, wild cavies and domesticated guinea pigs were presented with a 'water maze' puzzle, a test of spatial learning in which they had to find a hidden acrylic platform that would allow them to escape from a water-filled pool. Different geometric shapes made of black adhesive film were stuck to the inside of the pool, and gave clues to the platform's location. (On the face of it, this sounds cruel, or at the very least stressful. The scientists pointed out that the guinea pigs and cavies were good natural swimmers, were introduced to the apparatus 'gently' and were weighed regularly to ensure they were not losing condition. Animals that simply lay back and 'floated' – could these in fact have been the smartest ones? – were removed from the experiment.) Surprisingly, the domesticated guinea pigs performed better than the wild cavies, showing superior memory and spatial awareness skills. The researchers tentatively suggest that the 'reduced alertness, nervousness, and sensitivity of the domestic form is causally related to a reduction in the reactivity of the stress axes'. Because the guinea pigs had lower stress levels, and were generally more relaxed, learning and memory processes were given space to 'breathe' and to develop. Thus 'guinea pigs' domestication as an artificial selection for human desired traits did not lead to a degeneration of cognitive capabilities but rather to an adaptation to a man-made environment that allows solving the task even more efficiently.'[7]

From a human point of view, guinea pigs have been engineered to become just what we want them to be – a process which began

thousands of years ago in their Andean homeland, when the fiercer animals would have been dispatched more quickly, before they could breed, and which is still continuing today. Yet we could equally view this process the other way round, from the guinea pig's perspective, and conclude that, given the fact of captivity, guinea pigs have evolved in ways that are well suited to deal with their situation. Christine Künzl and Norbert Sachser write:

Camilla, Duchess of Cornwall, meets a guinea pig at Hackney City Farm, London.

> The following significant differences between wild cavies and domestic guinea pigs were found: the domesticated animals displayed less aggressive but more sociopositive and more male courtship behavior than their wild ancestors. In addition they were distinctly less attentive to their physical environment than the wild cavies . . . Thus, in

guinea pigs the process of domestication has led to typical
behavioral traits – reduced aggressiveness, increased social
tolerance – which have also been found in comparisons
between wild and domestic forms of other species.[8]

Male guinea pigs do occasionally fight with their rivals, but this
is relatively rare: a mutually understood code of vocalizations
and movements (such as the rumblestrutting described earlier)
usually prevents any actual violence. Given that they have no way
of escaping from close contact with their fellows, guinea pigs
have worked out sensible rules for coexistence.

However, the fact remains that collectively they are completely
under our thumb. This theme, of 'handling' for whatever purpose,
has been a constant in the guinea pig story. Their role, it seems,
is to be picked up and then set going, whether in the laboratory,
the show arena or in the numerous fictions that have been com-
posed around them. Perhaps the strangest of these fictions, and
one which asks us to reconsider the ways in which we approach
or distance ourselves from other creatures (including humans),
is Ludvík Vaculík's *The Guinea Pigs*.[9]

The Guinea Pigs is set in Prague, during Cold War Soviet rule.
The narrator, Vašek, has a quintessentially bureaucratic job in
the State Bank, arranging piles of banknotes 'with all the pictures facing the same way'. He and the other employees periodically
try to smuggle bundles of notes out of the building, and sometimes manage to evade the guards' searches. The image is of an
ill-regulated, shambolic system, always on the verge of collapse.

Vašek is charmed by his colleague Karásek's description of
the pet guinea pigs who run up his arms and perch on his shoulders, and he buys a guinea pig for his sons as a Christmas present.
Eventually there are several of them, and the female, Albínka, is
pregnant. At home, Vašek becomes absorbed in the animals'

A guinea pig joins in Mardi Gras festivities in Shreveport, Louisiana.

behaviour, monitoring them endlessly and observing their inter-actions. When a new guinea pig, Ruprecht, is introduced to the communal cage,

> he ran around a few times, apparently surprised that he had to turn so many corners . . . When he stumbled over Albínek sitting frozen in a corner, he sniffed his head, and then wanted to do the same honour to his opposite end, but he couldn't, because it was crammed in the corner . . . And then Ruprecht emitted a sort of pleasant sound, the like

of which we hadn't heard before. It was a gentle murmur
something like a cat's purr, but louder. It sounded more
like cooing . . . He lifted his rear end on his straddled legs,
raised himself up on his toes and began to step from one
foot to the other in a very comic manner. He looked like a
dandy in jodhpurs who arrives proudly at a ball, but is
oblivious of the fact that he left his boots at home.

If Vašek had limited himself to watching his guinea pigs all
would have been well, but the story quickly turns darker. He often
removes them from their cage so he can examine them more
closely, and then he begins to subject them to various ordeals. He
places Ruprecht on a revolving gramophone turntable, ostensibly
to find out the speed he prefers, and, more callously, puts him in
the bathtub while slowly filling it with water, all the time minutely
cataloguing his reactions. 'The guinea pig backed off and raised its
gaze even more intensely to the edge of the tub. It gave a nervous

Guinea pigs do
furnish a garden.

Adriaen van der
Werff, *Two Children
with a Guinea-pig
and a Kitten*,
c. 1681.

wink of its eye, or rather half of its face twitched. Its nose got
longer. It turned in place in rapid little leaps.' When Vašek exer-
cises his godlike power to save Ruprecht from drowning, he is
aware of 'a drunken excitement' that he had never known before.
'We're saved', he whispers to himself, as he holds the animal close.

Power corrupts; Vašek, who is just a number to his employers,
compensates by treating his sons harshly and his guinea pigs with

Guinea pigs often participate in Pets As Therapy schemes.

ingenious sadism. Yet he cannot distance himself from his animal victims. It is almost as if his obsessive handling of them blurs distinctions, for when one of them climbs on to his head he describes it as 'messing with my *fur*', and as he peers at the same animal close-up he seems to be studying the face of an equal: 'Its rabbity cleft displayed two shiny mouse-like teeth, its long white whiskers were quivering, and the pink fuzzy nostrils looked as if they were in a draught. Vašek becomes more and more paranoid, and the story spirals into the blacker realms of fantasy. By the end he has begun to refer to himself in the third person as 'the banker', and his final disappearance is both mysterious and sinister. However, Albínka and Ruprecht survive, and the novel ends with his sons playing with the babies that have just been born.

Vašek failed to find the right balance between involvement and detachment with regard to his guinea pigs. It could be argued that we are guilty of this too. Over the years we have inflicted much suffering on this species in the name of science. It, in turn, has given us a very great deal, not only enabling countless beneficial discoveries but delighting us with its quirks of behaviour and its gentle disposition. We cannot stop being gods, but we should be compassionate gods, using the knowledge we have gained to empathize and to protect. And we ought to remember that, although we look down on the guinea pig from above, it has kept some of its secrets: it *does* have a tail, in the form of coccygeal vertebrae – we just can't see it.

Timeline of the Guinea Pig

5000 BC	2800–1500 BC	AD 100–750	c. AD 1000
Guinea pigs first domesticated by tribes living in the Altiplano region of South America	Guinea pigs kept in tunnels in the coastal settlement of Huarmey, Peru	The Moche people keep guinea pigs in pens for consumption	Bodies of guinea pigs buried in a ritual context at the sacred site of Pachacamac, Peru

1610–15	1653	1777	1781
Felipe Guaman Poma de Ayala describes the Incas' sacrifice of guinea pigs to ensure good harvests	The English physician William Harvey uses guinea pigs in his anatomical investigations	Johann Christian Polycarp Erxleben gives the guinea pig its scientific name of *Cavia porcellus*	Thomas Pennant christens the guinea pig 'the restless cavy'

1929	1941	1970	1971
Beatrix Potter's *The Fairy Caravan* is published	The Guinea Pig Club is founded in East Grinstead, Sussex	Ludvík Vaculík's novel *The Guinea Pigs* is published	Michael Bond, *The Tales of Olga da Polga* is published

1526	1551	c. 1575	1610–12
Oviedo observes domesticated guinea pigs in Santo Domingo	Conrad Gesner describes the guinea pig in the first volume of his *Historiae animalium*	A guinea pig is kept at Hill Hall, Essex, by the Elizabethan statesman Thomas Smith	Peter Paul Rubens and Jan Brueghel the Elder include two guinea pigs in their *The Return from War: Mars Disarmed by Venus*

1882, 1883	1896	1907	1916
Robert Koch discovers the tuberculosis and cholera bacilli, with the aid of guinea pigs	Charles Cumberland's *Guinea Pigs and How to Keep Them* encourages the growth of a guinea pig 'fancy'	Axel Holst and Theodor Frølich use guinea pigs to demonstrate the importance of diet in the treatment of scurvy	William E. Castle and Sewall Wright publish *Studies of Inheritance in Guinea-pigs and Rats*, a major contribution to theories of inheritance

1977	1990	2009	2013
The British Cavy Council is founded	Peter Gurney starts to use guinea pigs as therapy for children in hospital	Researchers at La Molina University develop the large and fast-growing 'Peruvian Breed' for guinea pig farmers to export	The EU bans the marketing of all cosmetic products containing ingredients that have been tested on animals

References

1 WHAT'S IN A NAME?

1 'Pigs is Pigs' was first published in the *American Magazine* in 1905 and frequently anthologized after that. It may be read online at www.gutenberg.org. It was also made into a 10-minute cartoon by Walt Disney in 1954.

2 See ZSL, 'Santa Catarina's Guinea Pig (*Cavia intermedia*)', www.edgeofexistence.org, accessed 2 June 2014.

3 See Barbara J. Weir, 'Notes on the Origin of the Domestic Guinea Pig', in I. W. Rowlands and Barbara J. Weir, *The Biology of Hystricomorph Rodents* (New York, 1975).

4 Gonzalo Fernández de Oviedo, *Natural History of the West Indies*, trans. and ed. Sterling A. Stoudemire (Chapel Hill, NC, 1959), p. 18; Antonello Gerbi, *Nature in the New World: From Christopher Columbus to Gonzalo Fernández de Oviedo*, trans. Jeremy Moyle (Pittsburgh, PA, 1986), p. 294, n. 211.

5 William Harvey, *Anatomical Exercitations: Concerning the Generation of Living Creatures* (London, 1653), pp. 527–8.

6 C. A. Gmelig-Nijboer, *Conrad Gessner's 'Historia animalium': An Inventory of Renaissance Zoology* (Utrecht, 1977), pp. 69–70; Conrad Gesner, *Historiae animalium*, vol. 1 (Frankfurt, 1620), p. 367.

7 Thomas Pennant, *History of Quadrupeds* (London, 1781), pp. 361–2.

8 John Jeffrey-Cook, 'William Pitt and his Taxes', *British Tax Review*, 4 (2010), pp. 376–91.

9 Ray Puxley, *Britslang: An Uncensored A–Z of the People's Language, Including Rhyming Slang* (London, 2003).

10 Alexander Johnstone Wilson, *A Glossary of Colloquial, Slang and Technical Terms in Use on the Stock Exchange and in the Money Market* (London, 1895).

11 Edward Bishop, *McIndoe's Army: The Story of the Guinea Pig Club and its Indomitable Members* (London, 2001). A play, *The Guinea Pig Club*, by Susan Watkins, opened at York's Theatre Royal in 2012.

2 AT HOME IN THE ANDES

1 Daniel H. Sandweiss and Elizabeth S. Wing, 'Ritual Rodents: The Guinea Pigs of Chincha, Peru', *Journal of Field Archaeology*, XXIV/1 (1997), p. 49.

2 Peter W. Stahl, 'Pre-Columbian Andean Animal Domesticates at the Edge of Empire', *World Archaeology*, XXXIV/3 (2003), pp. 470–83.

3 E. Lanning, *Peru before the Incas* (Englewood Cliffs, NJ, 1967), p. 63; Sandweiss and Wing, 'Ritual Rodents', p. 49.

4 Garth Bawden, *The Moche* (Oxford, 1996), p. 82.

5 Lidio M. Valdez and J. Ernesto Valdez, 'Reconsidering the Archaeological Rarity of Guinea Pig Bones in the Central Andes', *Current Anthropology*, XXXVIII/5 (Chicago, IL, 1997), p. 897.

6 Nicolas Goepfert, *Frayer la route d'un monde inverse: sacrifice et offrandes animals dans la culture Mochica (100–800 apr. J.-C.), côte nord de Pérou*, Paris Monographs in American Archaeology, 28 (Oxford, 2011), pp. 160, 147.

7 Sandweiss and Wing, 'Ritual Rodents', p. 49.

8 Ibid.

9 A. E. Spotorno et al., 'Domestication of Guinea-pigs from a Southern Peru–Northern Chile Wild Species and their Middle Pre-Columbian Mummies', in *The Quintessential Naturalist: Honoring the Life and Legacy of Oliver P. Pearson*, ed. Douglas A. Kelt, Enrique P. Lessa, Jorge Salazar-Bravo and James L. Patton, University of California Publications in Zoology, vol. CXXXIV (Berkeley, CA, 2007), p. 380 and Plate II.

10 Ibid., p. 373 and Plate I.

11 Ibid., pp. 367, 382. See also J. P. Thorpe and J. Smartt, 'Genetic Diversity as a Component of Biodiversity', in *Global Biodiversity Assessment*, ed. R. T. Watson and V. H. Heywood (Cambridge and New York, 1995), pp. 57–87; and, for authoritative studies of the process of animal domestication, Juliet Clutton-Brock, *A Natural History of Domesticated Mammals* (Cambridge, 1999), and, most recently, *Animals as Domesticates: A World View through History* (East Lansing, MI, 2012).

12 Sandweiss and Wing, 'Ritual Rodents', pp. 51–2.

13 Ibid., p. 50.

14 Ibid.

15 Ibid.

16 Daniel W. Gade, 'The Guinea Pig in Andean Folk Culture', *Geographical Review*, LVII/2 (1967), p. 217.

17 Sandweiss and Wing, 'Ritual Rodents', p. 50.

18 Felipe Guaman Poma de Ayala, *The First New Chronicle and Good Government: On the History of the World and the Incas up to 1615*, ed. and trans. Roland Hamilton (Austin, TX, 2009), p. 189.

19 Ibid.

20 John Hemming, *The Search for El Dorado* (London, 1978), p. 85.

21 John Hemming, *The Conquest of the Incas* [1970] (London, 1993), p. 413.

22 Sandweiss and Wing, 'Ritual Rodents', p. 50.

23 Edmundo Morales, *The Guinea Pig: Healing, Food, and Ritual in the Andes* (Tucson, AZ, 1995), p. 99.

24 See Thom Belote, www.revthom.blogspot.co.uk/2012. A painting of 1656 in the convent of San Francisco in Lima shows the disciples eating guinea pig and drinking from gold Inca cups (*qeros*), while those in the cathedral in Quito, Ecuador (1802), include, as well as the guinea-pig feast, a Nativity scene with a llama peering over the crib. See also Morales, *Guinea Pig*, p. 100.

25 D. W. Gade, 'The Guinea Pig in Andean Folk Culture', *Geographical Review*, 57 (1967), p. 221.

26 Eduardo P. Archetti, *Guinea-Pigs: Food, Symbol and Conflict of Knowledge in Ecuador* (Oxford, 1997), pp. 16, 8, 4, 47, 32.

27 Quin Murray, pers. comm.

28 Morales, *The Guinea Pig*, pp. 13–14.

29 Archetti, *Guinea-pigs*, p. 108.

30 Morales, *The Guinea Pig*, p. 93.

31 Ibid., p. 95.

32 Ibid., pp. 81–6.

33 Ibid., pp. 95–6.

34 Ibid., pp. 104–5.

35 Ibid., pp. 123–5.

36 Archetti, *Guinea-pigs*, pp. 71–2, 73, 22.

37 Morales, *The Guinea Pig*, pp. 127–8, 131.

3 ARRIVING IN EUROPE

1 I have not been able to find a first-hand source for the Queen Elizabeth story, although it is very frequently repeated. Later in the chapter we will meet a guinea pig named Queen Elizabeth, owned by Beatrix Potter's friend Nina Paget, but it was probably named for the white ruff round its neck. The picture of the girl with a pet guinea pig is in private ownership. It was shown in the exhibition 'Elizabeth I and her People' at the National Portrait Gallery, 2013–14, and is reproduced in full colour and described in the book accompanying the exhibition: Tarnya Cooper with Jane Eade, *Elizabeth I and Her People* (London, 2013), pp. 108–9.

2 Paul Drury, with Richard Simpson, *Hill Hall: A Singular House Devised by a Tudor Intellectual* (The Society of Antiquaries of London, 2009), pp. 346–7.

3 Fabienne Pigière, Wim Van Neer, Cécile Ansieau and Marceline Denis, 'New Archaeozoological Evidence for the Introduction of the Guinea Pig to Europe', *Journal of Archaeological Science*, XXXIX/4 (April 2012), pp. 1020–24.

4 Arianne Faber Kolb, *Jan Brueghel the Elder: The Entry of the Animals into Noah's Ark* (Los Angeles, CA, 2005), p. 13; Anne T. Woollett

and Ariane van Suchtelen, eds, *Rubens and Brueghel: A Working Friendship* (Zwolle, 2006), p. 70.

5 Kolb, *Jan Brueghel the Elder*, p. 49.

6 Woollett and van Suchtelen, eds, *Rubens and Brueghel*, p. 55.

7 Ibid., p. 56.

8 *The Guardian*, No. 106 (13 July 1713).

9 George Edwards, *Gleanings of Natural History, Exhibiting Figures of Quadrupeds, Birds, Fishes, Insects, etc.*, part 2 (London, 1760), p. 180.

10 Ibid., p. 181.

11 Oliver Goldsmith, *An History of the Earth and Animated Nature*, vol. IV (London, 1774), pp. 55–63.

12 Thomas Bewick, *A General History of Quadrupeds*, 3rd edn (London, 1792), pp. 345–6.

13 Isabella Beeton, *Beeton's Book of Home Pets* (London, 1862), p. 698.

14 Isabella Beeton, *The Book of Household Management* (London, 1861), §997.

15 *The Chip Boy; or, Grandpapa's Story about a Plumcake, and Other Stories* (London, *c*. 1880), pp. 68–88.

16 From *Fun for the Holidays* (New York [*c*.1887]), p. 60.

17 William Lingard, 'Italian Guinea Pig Boy', words and music (London [1866]).

18 James Greenwood, *In Strange Company: Being the Experiences of a Roving Correspondent*, 2nd edn (London, 1874), p. 79, at www.victorianlondon.org.

19 *The Journal of Beatrix Potter, 1881–1897*, transcribed from her code writings by Leslie Linder (Harmondsworth, 1989).

20 Judy Taylor, *Beatrix Potter: Artist, Storyteller and Countrywoman* (Harmondsworth, 1986), p. 160.

21 Charles Cumberland, *Guinea Pigs and How to Keep Them* (London, 1896), p. 2.

22 Ibid., pp. 2, 7.

23 Ibid., pp. 20, 21.

24 Ibid., p. 71.

25 Ibid., pp. 7, 58

26 Ibid., pp. 89, 88–96.
27 Ibid., p. 91.

4 ON THE MENU

1 'At Least It Wasn't a Gopher! Phillip Schofield Sparks Outrage
   after Boasting about Eating Guinea Pig', *Daily Mirror*, 5 November
   2012; interview on *This Morning* (ITV), broadcast 6 November
   2012. Schofield's previous work in children's TV, particularly
   with a puppet sidekick called Gordon the Gopher, apparently
   compounded his offence.
2 *Wild Shepherdess with Kate Humble: Peru*, first broadcast
   28 June 2013 (BBC2).
3 Lynn Levin, 'How to Eat a Pet: A Gastronomic Adventure in the
   Andes', first published in *Alimentum: The Literature of Food*, 2
   (Summer 2006). Republished as 'How to Eat a Guinea Pig',
   in *The Economist*'s online magazine *More Intelligent Life*,
   www.moreintelligentlife.com.
4 See 'Christian Cookbook Roasted over Guinea Pig Recipe',
   Austrian Times, 20 April 2009.
5 Edmundo Morales, *The Guinea Pig: Healing, Food, and Ritual in the
   Andes* (Tucson, AZ, 1995), p. 57.
6 Ibid., pp. 16–20.
7 'Peru Pushes Guinea Pigs as Food', *CBS News*, 11 February 2009;
   'Guinea Pig: It's What's for Dinner in Peru – and the U.S.',
   Christian Science Monitor, 1 November 2006.
8 Edmundo Morales, pers. comm.
9 Eduardo P. Archetti, *Guinea-pigs: Food, Symbol and Conflict of
   Knowledge in Ecuador* (Oxford, 1997), p. 126, n. 4.
10 National Public Radio, 'The Salt', www.npr.org/blogs, 12 March 2013.
11 Ibid.
12 *Microlivestock: Little-known Animals with a Promising Economic
   Future*, Office of International Affairs (1991), pp. 240–49.
13 Charles Cumberland, *Guinea Pigs and How to Keep Them*
   (London, 1896), p. 33.

14 Ibid., p. 44.

15 Ibid., p. 34.

16 Isabella Beeton, *The Book of Household Management* (London, 1861), §997.

17 'Guinea Pig Power', www.wanderinggaia.com, 5 September 2010.

5 EXPERIMENTAL SUBJECTS

1 Jim Endersby, *A Guinea Pig's History of Biology: The Plants and Animals who Taught us the Facts of Life* (London, 2007), p. 236. Chapter 7, '*Cavia porcellus*: Mathematical Guinea Pigs', is a thought-provoking and thoroughly entertaining account of all that biologists owe to guinea pigs, and this chapter is greatly indebted to it.

2 See Anita Guerrini, *Experimenting with Humans and Animals: From Galen to Animal Rights* (Baltimore, 2003), pp. 42–3.

3 Leonora Cohen Rosenfield, *From Beast-Machine to Man-Machine* [1940] (New York, 1968), p. 64.

4 William Harvey, *Anatomical Exercitations: Concerning the Generation of Living Creatures* (London, 1653), pp. 527–8.

5 Charles Raven, *John Ray, Naturalist: His Life and Works* (Cambridge, 1942), p. 375.

6 See Guerrini, *Experimenting with Humans and Animals*, pp. 70, 87.

7 See Endersby, *A Guinea Pig's History of Biology*, pp. 217–19.

8 See Guerrini, *Experimenting with Humans and Animals*, p. 108.

9 Charles Darwin, *The Variation of Animals and Plants under Domestication*, 2 vols (London, 1868), vol. II, p. 24.

10 See R. Wheatley, 'Hygeia in Manhattan', *Harper's New Monthly Magazine* (February 1897), pp. 384–401, 386.

11 Paul de Kruif, *Microbe Hunters*, The Life and Letters Series No. 3 (London, 1930), pp. 206–7, 212.

12 Sinclair Lewis, *Arrowsmith* (New York, 1925); quoted in Endersby, *A Guinea Pig's History of Biology*, pp. 251–2.

13 Kenneth J. Carpenter, *The History of Scurvy and Vitamin C* (Cambridge, 1986), p. 176; for a full history of the role of guinea

pigs, see chapter Eight, and Endersby, *A Guinea Pig's History of Biology*, pp. 220–25.

14 Endersby, *A Guinea Pig's History of Biology*, pp. 236–7.

15 Ibid., p. 242. The story is told in an interview of 1996 with Robert E. Sloan conducted by Joe Cain, at www.ucl.ac.uk/sts/staff/cain/projects. However, Sloan heard of the incident at second hand, through a friend, and Wright himself always denied that it ever happened.

16 W. E. Castle and Sewall Wright, *Studies of Inheritance in Guinea-pigs and Rats* (Washington, DC, 1916), p. 31.

17 Naomi Mitchison, 'Beginnings', in *Haldane and Modern Biology*, ed. K. M. Dronamraju (Baltimore, MD, 1968), p. 303.

18 Endersby, *A Guinea Pig's History of Biology*, pp. 232–3.

19 'Look At These Skinny Pigs!', *The Sun*, 18 October 2007.

6 PETS, PLAIN AND FANCY

1 William S. Fortey, *How to Manage Rabbits* (London, n.d.).

2 Ibid.

3 Charles Cumberland, *Guinea Pigs and How to Keep Them* (London, 1896), p. 64.

4 Sir Robert Heron, *Notes: Printed but not Published* (Grantham, 1850), pp. 201–2.

5 Cumberland, *Guinea Pigs and How to Keep Them*, p. 51.

6 Wellesley Pain, *Rabbits: Guinea-pigs: Fancy Mice* (London, 1938), p. 57.

7 Cumberland, *Guinea Pigs and How to Keep Them*, p. 17.

8 At www.petergurney.com, accessed 1 January 2015.

9 Peter Gurney, *Piggy Potions: Natural Remedies for Guinea Pigs* (Havant, 1995).

10 Peter Gurney, 'Obituary', *Daily Telegraph*, 8 July 2006.

11 Joseph Bucklin Bishop, ed., *Theodore Roosevelt's Letters to his Children* (New York, 1919), p. 19. There is a possibly apocryphal story that Roosevelt was in a meeting when he was interrupted by one of his children bursting in and shouting, 'Father, come quickly! Bishop Doane has just had babies!'

12 The Peter Gurney Guinea Pig Health Guide, at
www.oginet.com/pgurney/barbering, accessed 4 June 2014.

13 Peter Gurney, *Guinea Pig: A Practical Guide to Caring for your Guinea Pig* (London, 1999), p. 79.

14 'Breed Standards for Full and Guide Standard Cavies',
www.britishcavycouncil.org.uk, accessed 2 June 2014. Subsequent quotes are from the same source, unless otherwise noted; emphases (italics) are in the original.

15 Margaret Elward and Mette Ruelokke, *Guinea Piglopaedia: A Complete Guide to Guinea Pig Care* (Dorking, 2003), p. 145.

16 See Wynne Eecen, *Pigs Isn't Pigs* (Sydney, 1974).

7 HEROES AND HEROINES

1 *The Tale of Tuppenny* first appeared in 1971, in *A History of the Writings of Beatrix Potter*. A new edition, with illustrations by Marie Angel (there are no pictures by Potter herself), was published by Frederick Warne in 1973.

2 Paul Gallico, *The Day the Guinea-Pig Talked* (London, 1963), p. 18.

3 Michael Bond, *Bears and Forebears: A Life So Far* (London, 1996), p. 174.

4 Ibid., p. 176.

5 Catherine Rayner, pers. comm., June 2013.

6 David Ellison, speaking in 'Paws, Claws and Videotape', broadcast 2 March 2010, BBC4.

7 Heinlein Society, 'FAQ: Frequently Asked Questions about Robert A. Heinlein, his Works', www.heinleinsociety.org, accessed 2 June 2014. The entire tribble saga is related in David Gerrold, *The Trouble with Tribbles: Full Story of the Classic Star Trek Show* (London, 1996).

8 Cuddly Cavies Creations: www.cuddlycavies.homestead.com; Maki Yamada's website is www.guineapigfashion.com.

1 Michael Bond, *The Tales of Olga da Polga* (Oxford, 2006), chapter Four, 'Olga's Story'.

2 Caspar Henderson, *The Book of Barely Imagined Beings: A 21st-century Bestiary* (London, 2012), pp. xviii–xix.

3 Dan Graur, Winston A. Hide, and Wen-Hsiung Li, 'Is the Guinea-pig a Rodent?', *Nature*, 351 (20 June 1991), pp. 648–52; see also Anne-Maria d'Erchia et al., 'The Guinea-pig is Not a Rodent', *Nature*, 381 (13 June 1996), pp. 597–600.

4 Thomas Bewick, *A General History of Quadrupeds*, 3rd edn (London, 1792), p. 345.

5 H. W. Brands, *TR: The Last Romantic* (New York, 1997), pp. 712, 577.

6 J. Allen, 'The Associative Processes of the Guinea Pig: A Study of the Psychical Development of an Animal with a Nervous System Well Medullated at Birth', *Journal of Comparative Neurology and Psychology*, xiv/4 (1904), p. 293.

7 Lars Lewejohann, Thorsten Pickel, Norbert Sachser, and Sylvia Kaiser, 'Wild Genius – Domestic Fool? Spatial Learning Abilities of Wild and Domestic Guinea Pigs', *Frontiers in Zoology*, vii/9 (2012), pp. 1–8.

8 Christine Künzl and Norbert Sachser, 'The Behavioral Endocrinology of Domestication: A Comparison between the Domestic Guinea Pig (*Cavia aperea porcellus*) and its Wild Ancestor, the Cavy (*Cavia aperea*)', *Hormones and Behavior*, xxxv/1 (1999), p. 28.

9 Ludvík Vaculík, *The Guinea Pigs*, trans. Káča Poláčková (London, 1976).

Select Bibliography

Allen, J., 'The Associative Processes of the Guinea Pig: A Study of the Psychical Development of an Animal with a Nervous System Well Medullated at Birth', *Journal of Comparative Neurology and Psychology*, xvi/4 (1904), pp. 293–359

Archetti, Eduardo P., *Guinea-pigs: Food, Symbol and Conflict of Knowledge in Ecuador*, trans. Valentina Napolitano and Peter Worsley (Oxford, 1997)

Birmelin, Immanuel, *My Guinea Pig and Me* (New York, 2001)

Bolton, R., 'Guinea Pigs, Protein, and Ritual', *Ethnology*, xviii/3 (1979), pp. 229–52

Brothwell, Don, 'Why on Earth the Guinea-Pig? The Problem of Restricted Mammal Exploitation in the New World', *BAR International Series*, 173 (Oxford, 1983), pp. 115–19

Care for your Guinea Pig, RSPCA Pet Guide (London, 2004)

Castle, W. E., and Sewall Wright, *Studies of Inheritance in Guinea-pigs and Rats* (Washington, DC, 1916)

Clutton-Brock, Juliet, *Animals as Domesticates: A World View through History* (East Lansing, MI, 2012)

—, *A Natural History of Domesticated Mammals* (Cambridge, 1999)

Cooper, G., and A. L. Schiller, *Anatomy of the Guinea Pig* (Cambridge, MA, 1975)

Cumberland, Charles, *Guinea Pigs and How to Keep Them* (London, 1896)

Eecen, Wynne, *Pigs Isn't Pigs* (Sydney, 1974)

Elward, Margaret, and Mette Ruelokke, *The Guinea Piglopaedia: A Complete Guide to Guinea Pigs* (Dorking, 2003)

Endersby, Jim, *A Guinea Pig's History of Biology: The Plants and Animals who Taught us the Facts of Life* (London, 2007)

Gade, D. W., 'The Guinea Pig in Andean Folk Culture', *Geographical Review*, 57 (1967), pp. 213–24.

Guerrini, Anita, *Experimenting with Humans and Animals: From Galen to Animal Rights* (Baltimore, MD, 2003)

Guidry, Virginia Parker, *Guinea Pigs: Practical Advice for Caring for your Guinea Pig* (Irvine, CA, 2004)

Gurney, Peter, *All of Their Kind* (self-published, 2002)

—, *Guinea Pig: A Practical Guide to Caring for your Guinea Pig* (London, 1999)

—, *Piggy Potions: Natural Remedies for Guinea Pigs* (Havant, Hampshire, 1995)

Künzl, Christine, and Norbert Sachser, 'The Behavioral Endocrinology of Domestication: A Comparison between the Domestic Guinea Pig (*Cavia aperea porcellus*) and its Wild Ancestor, the Cavy (*Cavia aperea*)', *Hormones and Behavior*, XXXV/1 (1999), pp. 28–37

Lewejohann, Lars, Thorsten Pickel, Norbert Sachser and Sylvia Kaiser, 'Wild Genius – Domestic Fool? Spatial Learning Abilities of Wild and Domestic Guinea Pigs', *Frontiers in Zoology*, VII/9 (2012), pp. 1–8

Mahoney, Myra, *Mini-encyclopedia of Guinea Pigs: Breeds and Care* (Dorking, 2010)

Mancini, Julie, *Guinea Pigs* (Dorking, 2008)

Mitchell, Chip, 'Guinea Pig: It's What's for Dinner in Peru – and the U.S.', *Christian Science Monitor*, 1 November 2006

Morales, Edmundo, 'The Guinea Pig in the Andean Economy: From Household Animal to Market Commodity', *Latin American Research Review*, XXIX/3 (1994), pp. 129–42

—, *The Guinea Pig: Healing, Food, and Ritual in the Andes* (Tucson, AZ, 1995)

Müller-Haye, B., 'Guinea-pig or Cuy', in *Evolution of Domesticated Animals* (London, 1984)

Pigière, Fabienne, et al., 'New Archaeozoological Evidence for the Introduction of the Guinea Pig to Europe', *Journal of Archaeological Science*, XXXIX/4 (April 2012), pp. 1020–24

Pritt, S., 'The History of the Guinea Pig (*Cavia porcellus*) in Society and Veterinary Medicine', *Veterinary Heritage* (1998), pp. 12–16

Reid, Mary Elizabeth, *The Guinea Pig in Research: Biology, Nutrition, Physiology* (Washington, DC, 1958)

Rosenfeld, Silvana A., 'Delicious Guinea Pigs: Seasonality Studies and the Use of Fat in the Pre-Columbian Andean Diet', *Quaternary International*, CLXXX/1 (2008), pp. 127–34

Sachser, Norbert, 'Of Domestic and Wild Guinea Pigs: Studies in Sociophysiology, Domestication, and Social Evolution', *Naturwissenschaften*, 85 (1998), pp. 307–17

Sandweiss, D. H., and E. S. Wing, 'Ritual Rodents: The Guinea Pigs of Chincha, Peru', *Journal of Field Archaeology*, 24 (1997), pp. 47–58

Spotorno, A. E., et al., 'Ancient and Modern Steps during the Domestication of Guinea Pigs (*Cavia porcellus* L.)', *Journal of Zoology*, 270 (2006), pp. 57–62

—, et al., 'Domestication of Guinea-pigs from a Southern Peru–Northern Chile Wild Species and their Middle Pre-Columbian Mummies', in *The Quintessential Naturalist: Honoring the Life and Legacy of Oliver P. Pearson*, ed. Douglas A. Kelt et al., (Berkeley, CA, 2007), pp. 367–88

Stahl, Peter W., 'Pre-Columbian Andean Animal Domesticates at the Edge of Empire', *World Archaeology*, XXXIV/3 (2003), pp. 470–83

Turner, Isabel, *Exhibition and Pet Cavies* (Liss, Hampshire, 1977)

Valdez, Lidio M., and J. Ernesto Valdez, 'Reconsidering the Archaeological Rarity of Guinea Pig Bones in the Central Andes', *Current Anthropology*, XXXVIII/5 (Chicago, IL, 1997), pp. 896–8

Vecchio, Rick, 'Peru Pushes Guinea Pigs as Food', *CBS News*, 11 February 2009

Wagner, J. E., and P. J. Manning, *The Biology of the Guinea Pig* (New York, 1976)

Weir, Barbara J., 'Notes on the Origin of the Domestic Guinea Pig', in I. W. Rowlands and Barbara J. Weir, *The Biology of Hystricomorph Rodents* (New York, 1975)

Associations and Websites

American Cavy Breeders Association
www.acbaonline.com

The British Cavy Council
www.britishcavycouncil.org.uk

The Cambridge Cavy Trust
www.britishassociationofrodentologists.co.uk/CCT

Guinea Pig Magazine
www.guineapigmagazine.com

National Cavy Club
www.nationalcavyclub.co.uk

The Scottish National Cavy Club
www.thescottishnationalcavyclub.weebly.com

Southern Cavy Club
www.southerncavyclub.co.uk

The Welsh National Cavy Club
wncc.moonfruit.com

Acknowledgements

Many people have generously shared their knowledge of guinea pigs with me or have otherwise helped my research. I would like to thank the staff of the Bodleian Library, Sackler Library, Radcliffe Science Library and the zsl Library, especially Ann Sylph; and also the volunteers at the East Grinstead Museum. Thanks to Monica Hawkes of the Anglo Peruvian Society, John Hemming, Elizabeth Knowles, Lynn Levin, Mike, Alex and Ruth McCarthy, Edmundo Morales, Debbie Protheroe and Gaia Vince for various kinds of assistance. I am extremely grateful to George and Eve DeLange, Juha Koivula, Laurent Lhomond, Fabienne Pigière and Maki Yamada for allowing me to reproduce their pictures – as I am to all the people who have generously made their photographs available by Commons licences. Special thanks to Quin Murray for sharing his experiences in Peru and allowing me to reproduce a picture from his website, and to Debbie Johnston of Glenwhilk Cavies for photographs of her beautiful animals.

Photo Acknowledgements

The author and publishers wish to express their thanks to the following sources of illustrative material and/or permission to reproduce it.

Photo Alexander Turnbull Library, Wellington, New Zealand: p. 22; courtesy of the author: pp. 15, 23, 24, 99, 108, 116, 117, 148, 149 (top), 156; Bridgeman Art Library: p. 92; British Museum, London (photos © Trustees of the British Museum): pp. 57, 62, 151, 157; photos © Trustees of the British Museum, London: pp. 19, 20, 64, 67; photo © chungking/Shutterstock.com: p. 149 (bottom); from Charles Cumberland, *Guinea Pigs and How to Keep Them* (London, 1896): pp. 71, 110, 111; photo John Cummings/CIAT: p. 85; photo George and Eve DeLange: p. 45; photo © W. Disney/Everett/Rex Features: p. 143; photo © Pierre-Jean Durieu/Shutterstock.com: p. 78 (left); from George Edwards, *Gleanings of Natural History . . .*, vol. II (London, 1760): p. 54; from Conrad Gesner, *Historiae animalium*, vol. I (Zurich, 1551): p. 12; courtesy Debbie Johnston, Glenwhilk Cavies: pp. 119, 120, 121, 122, 123; illustration copyright © Hans Helweg 1971, from Michael Bond, *The Tales of Olga da Polga* (Oxford, 1971), reproduced by permission of Oxford University Press: p. 135; The J. Paul Getty Museum, Los Angeles (digital images courtesy of the Getty's Open Content Program): pp. 51 (Jan Brueghel the Elder, *The Entry of the Animals into Noah's Ark*, 1613, oil on panel, size unframed 54.6 × 83.8 cm. Digital image courtesy of the Getty's Open Content Program), 52, 53 (Peter Paul Rubens and Jan Brueghel the Elder, *The Return from War: Mars Disarmed by Venus*, c. 1610–12, oil on panel, size

Index